READING
TO
BASINGSTOKE

Vic Mitchell and Keith Smith

MP Middleton Press

First published March 1994

ISBN 1 873793 27 8

© Middleton Press 1993

Design - Deborah Goodridge
Typesetting - Barbara Mitchell
             Deborah Goodridge

Published by Middleton Press
             Easebourne Lane
             Midhurst
             West Sussex
             GU29 9AZ
             Tel: (0730) 813169
(From 16 April 1995 - (01730) 813169)

Printed & bound by Biddles Ltd,
             Guildford and Kings Lynn

INDEX

ACKNOWLEDGEMENTS

Thanks are gratefully expressed to those mentioned in the photographic credits. They have been of great assistance as have J.H.Aston, R.S.Carpenter, G.Croughton, S.P.Derek, S.Geeson, P.Hay, M.King, N.Langridge, A.Ll.Lambert, Mr D. and Dr S.Salter, R.Silsbury, N.Sprinks, N.Stanyon, Miss M. Wheeller, Dr. R.W.Wille and our ever helpful wives.

Route diagram for 1908-22
(Railway World)

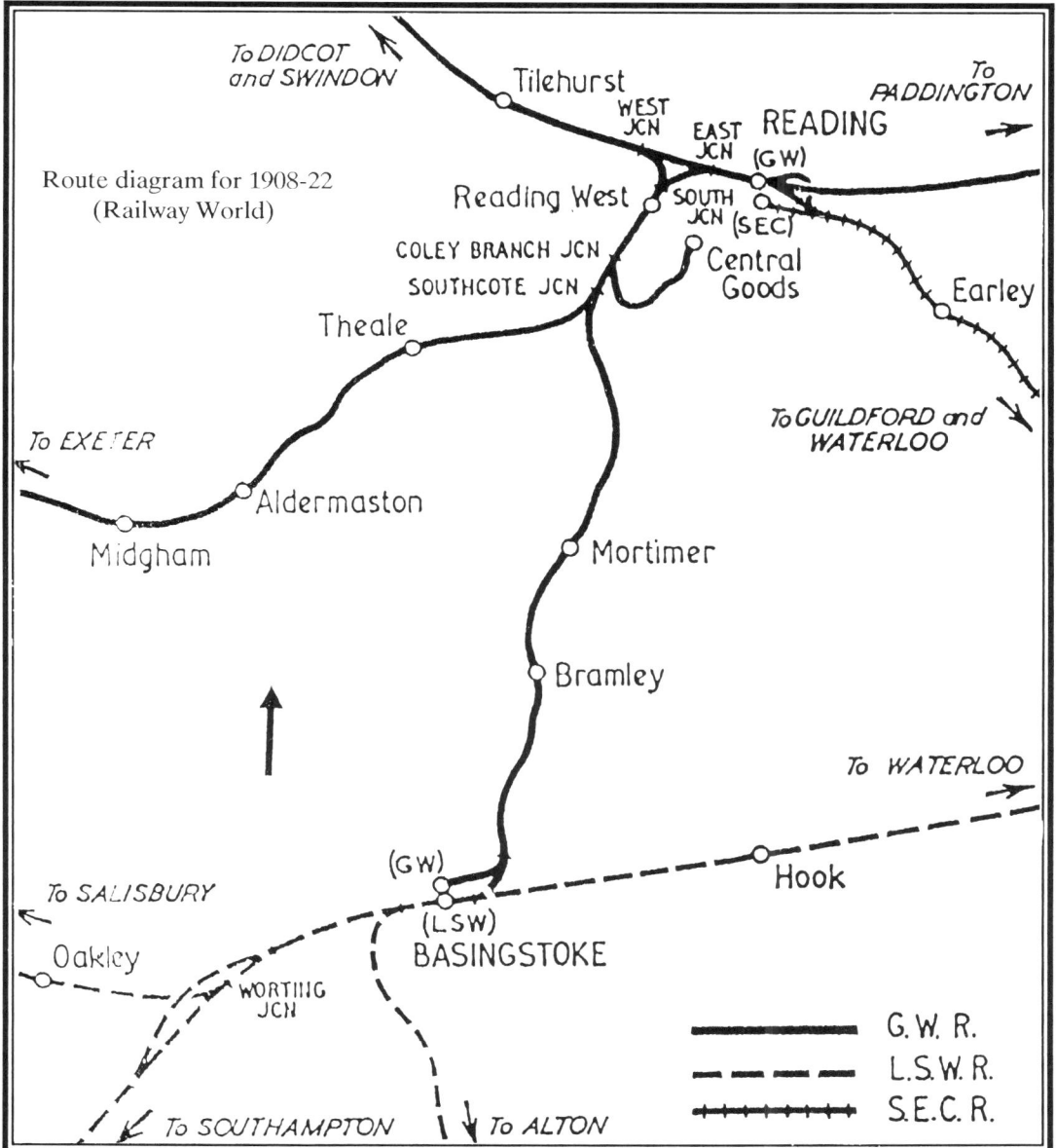

To DIDCOT and SWINDON

To PADDINGTON

Tilehurst

WEST JCN

EAST JCN

READING (GW)

Reading West

SOUTH JCN (SEC)

COLEY BRANCH JCN

SOUTHCOTE JCN

Central Goods

Earley

Theale

To GUILDFORD and WATERLOO

To EXETER

Aldermaston

Midgham

Mortimer

Bramley

To WATERLOO

(GW)

Hook

To SALISBURY

(LSW)

BASINGSTOKE

Oakley

WORTING JCN

To SOUTHAMPTON

To ALTON

———	G. W. R.
– – –	L.S.W. R.
+++++	S.E.C. R.

GEOGRAPHICAL SETTING

Reading is situated at the confluence of the Rivers Thames and Kennet, the main station being located close to the former. The route crosses the latter two miles south of the town shortly after diverging from the Newbury line at Southcote Junction.

For the first four miles the line is on alluvium and valley gravels and is then predominantly on London Clay to within one mile of Basingstoke, which is situated on Upper Chalk.

As far as Bramley, the streams close to the route flow north into the Kennet. The final two miles of our journey are now within the urban area of Basingstoke.

The maps are to the scale of 25" to 1 mile, unless otherwise stated.

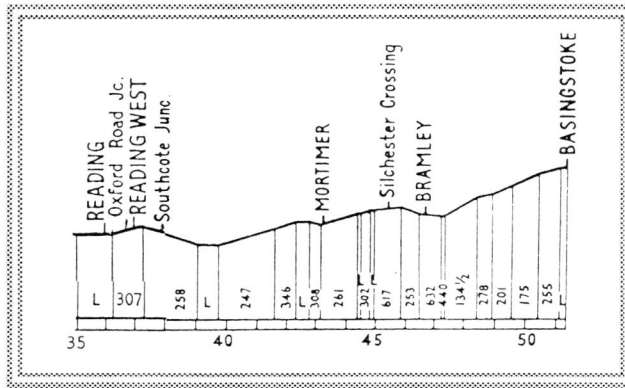

HISTORICAL BACKGROUND

The Great Western Railway's route from London reached Reading from Twyford on 30th April 1840 and was extended to Steventon on 1st June of that year, reaching Bristol in the following year. It was broad gauge.

Reading had already become an important centre for the corn trade, partly due to the opening of the Kennet & Avon Canal in 1810.

To the south, the London & South Western Railway reached Basingstoke from Winchfield on 10th June 1839 and was completed to Winchester on 11th May 1840. This was built to standard gauge.

The broad gauge Berks & Hants Railway of the GWR was authorised in 1845. The Reading-Hungerford section was opened on 21st December 1847 and the Basingstoke branch came into use on 1st November 1848.

With the lines of the South of England and those north of Oxford being standard gauge, the GWR inevitably had to add a third rail to their tracks to accommodate through traffic between these regions. This was completed on 22nd December 1856 along with a triangular

junction at Reading to eliminate the need for reversal there. The extra rails were not laid to the station at that time. Mixed gauge track through the station to connect with the South Eastern Railway's 1849 line was brought into use on 1st December 1858. (The link ran north of the platforms and passed under the GWR main line in a tunnel). Additional rails were laid later to Paddington, standard gauge services commencing on 1st October 1861. The outer rail was lifted on the branch in 1869 and the last broad gauge train on the GWR ran on 20th May 1892.

The final development of the railway system of the area took place on 4th May 1908 when the Coley Branch to Reading Central Goods Depot opened. It closed on 25th July 1983.

The route became part of the Western Region of British Railways upon nationalisation in 1948 but most of it was transferred to the Southern Region on 12th April 1950. It became part of Network SouthEast in 1986.

PASSENGER SERVICES

The following notes refer to down trains, this term applying to the Reading-Basingstoke direction. The summary table below gives an indication of the development of services, the examples being given about every 21 years. The description **Local** refers to trains starting at Reading although some continued to Portsmouth, Southampton or Salisbury. The heading **Through** indicates services from the Midlands or beyond to the South Coast and running on five or more days per week.

	Local		Through	
	Weekdays	Sundays	Weekdays	Sundays
1848	4	-	-	-
1869	6	1	-	-
1890	12	2	-	-
1911	10	3	1	-
1932	15	4	3	-
1953	13	7	2	-
1974	19	16	3	1
1994	35	17	8	4

Most local trains have called at all intermediate stations although at quiet times some have been omitted. In recent years all have been closed on Sunday mornings.

Through trains between Oxford and Basingstoke were started in 1891 and in 1902 they were extended to run between Newcastle and Bournemouth.

In 1905, departures from Basingstoke included through coaches to Paddington at 8.26am and to Windsor & Eton at 4.35pm. By 1911 return from London was at 7.30pm, by means of a slip coach.

Many extras were operated on summer Saturdays - for example there were fourteen on such days in 1958. Southern destinations have included Portsmouth Harbour, Stokes Bay, Southampton Terminus, Bournemouth West and Weymouth, while northern towns to be reached range from Newcastle and Birkenhead, to Derby and Nottingham. Scottish cities have been added to the list in recent years.

The "Pines Express" was well known on the Somerset & Dorset line as the Manchester-Bournemouth direct service. It was changed to run via Reading West from September 1962 until its demise in June 1967, although from the autumn of 1966 all through trains reversed at Reading. The decline in inter-regional working was arrested in 1972 when destinations and frequency of the long distance trains using the route was increased.

There are two notable dates in the history of local service improvements. Firstly, 9th September 1962 saw the introduction of a basic hourly service, provided by diesel electric multiple units (DEMUs). Secondly, from 2nd October 1989 passengers had the benefit of a half hourly interval timetable, this being operated by Turbo diesels from May 1993. Few routes have seen such improvements in recent years.

READING and BASINGSTOKE.

[timetable - Reading and Basingstoke, Week Days and Sundays, Down and Up services]

April 1932

READING

1. The first station comprised an up platform (in the distance) and a down platform (behind the camera), *both on the down line* (right). Both platforms had roofs over them and the two adjacent tracks, the up station roof being featured here. The main lines are to the left of the roof. The two platforms were linked in 1861 but mixed gauge track was not laid at them until 1869. This photograph was taken after 1892 but before 1896. Construction of the building on the right was started in 1865; it displaced the original down buildings and both up and down goods sheds, which had been between the platforms. (Lens of Sutton)

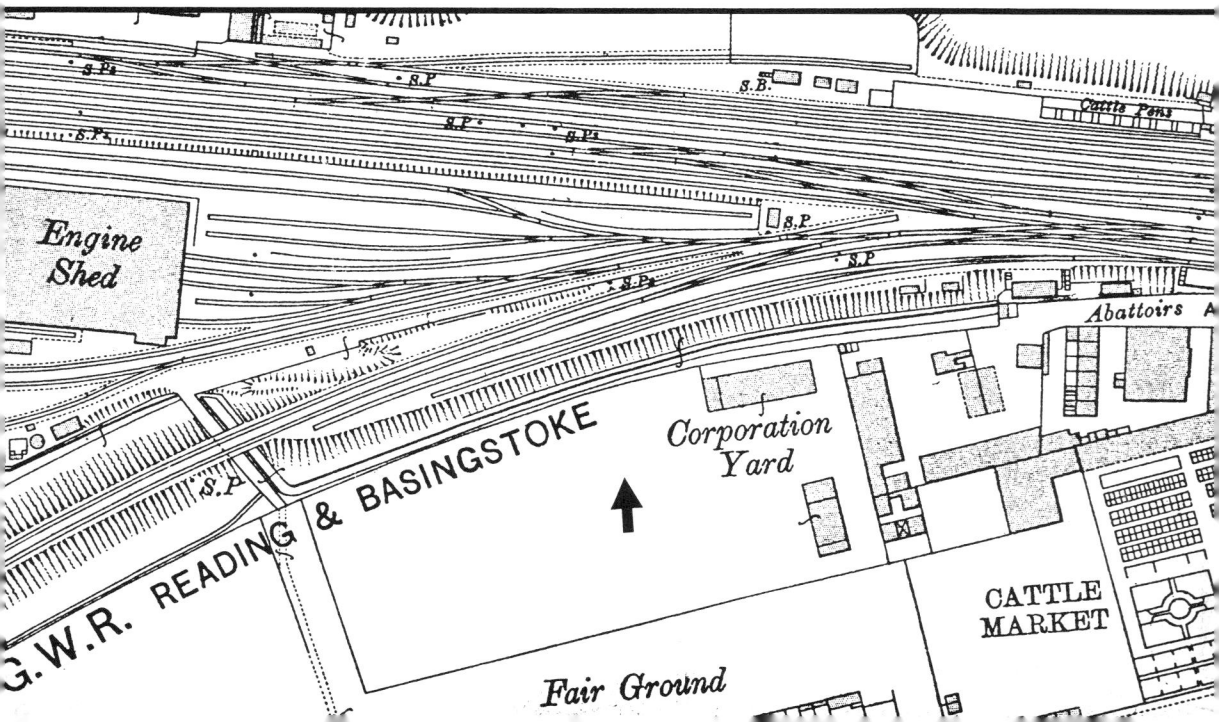

2. This impressive structure with its Italianate frontage served as the town's main station building for over a century. Finished in 1868, it still stands today although a new passenger entrance has been in use since 1989. Additional platforms had been provided in 1861 to accommodate standard gauge trains and more were added in 1899. At this time there were over 300 trains serving the station on weekdays and there were more than 200 uniformed staff. (Lens of Sutton)

The 1912 survey includes the bays at the west end of the station only. The map of the east end is below pictures 2 and 3 in our *Reading to Guildford* album, which also features the SER station and its later developments.

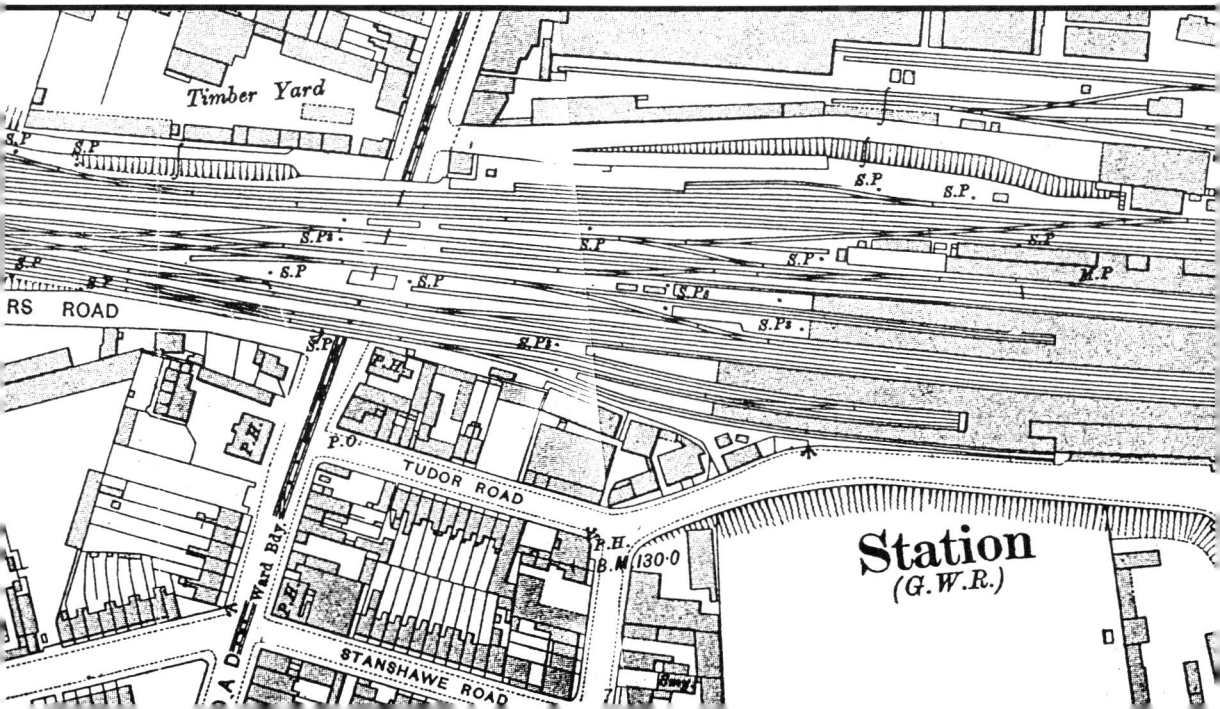

Station
(G.W.R.)

3. The SR operated some of the local Reading-Basingstoke services. In 1934 these amounted to 3 out of 16 trains. Ex-LSWR class M7 no. 111 is being coupled to a coach of similar origin in what was then termed platform 1 West Bay. (Lens of Sutton)

4. Viewed from West Main Box in 1953, the Basingstoke branch curves to the left, between the two carriage sidings and the engine shed. "Britannia" class 4-6-2 no. 70025 *Western Star* is London-bound with the "The Red Dragon" from Wales. (M.W.Earley/National Railway Museum)

5. Seen from the same signal box and in the same year (the headboards carry the new monarch's initials and crown), the down "Cornish Riviera" departs west and is signalled to Reading West. In the background horse boxes stand at the dock from which Motorail services departed to Fishguard and St.Austell from March 1967. (M.W.Earley/National Railway Museum)

7. A local train for Basingstoke on 17th August 1954 was hauled by class N15X no. 32328. It is standing at platform 2 which was the only one not to be renumbered in the following year. (R.M.Casserley)

6. The sign in front of Middle Box proclaims "Reading General". This name was in use from 26th September 1949 until 6th May 1973. The number of platforms was increased from four to ten in 1899, in association with the quadrupling of the main line. The adjacent table reveals the complex numbering in use until 1955. (Lens of Sutton)

1899	1955
1 (dn. main)	4
1 West Bay	3
2 (*bay*)	2
3 (*bay*)	1
4 (*centre*)	5
5 (*island*)	8
4 East Bay	6
4 West Bay	7
6 (*up relief*)	9
6 East Bay	10

8. In absence of crossovers, engines were trapped at the buffers until their train was taken away by another or they propelled the coaches into one of the sidings seen on the left of picture no.4. No. 1 road was later shortened so that its buffers are now level with nos. 2 and 3. (Lens of Sutton)

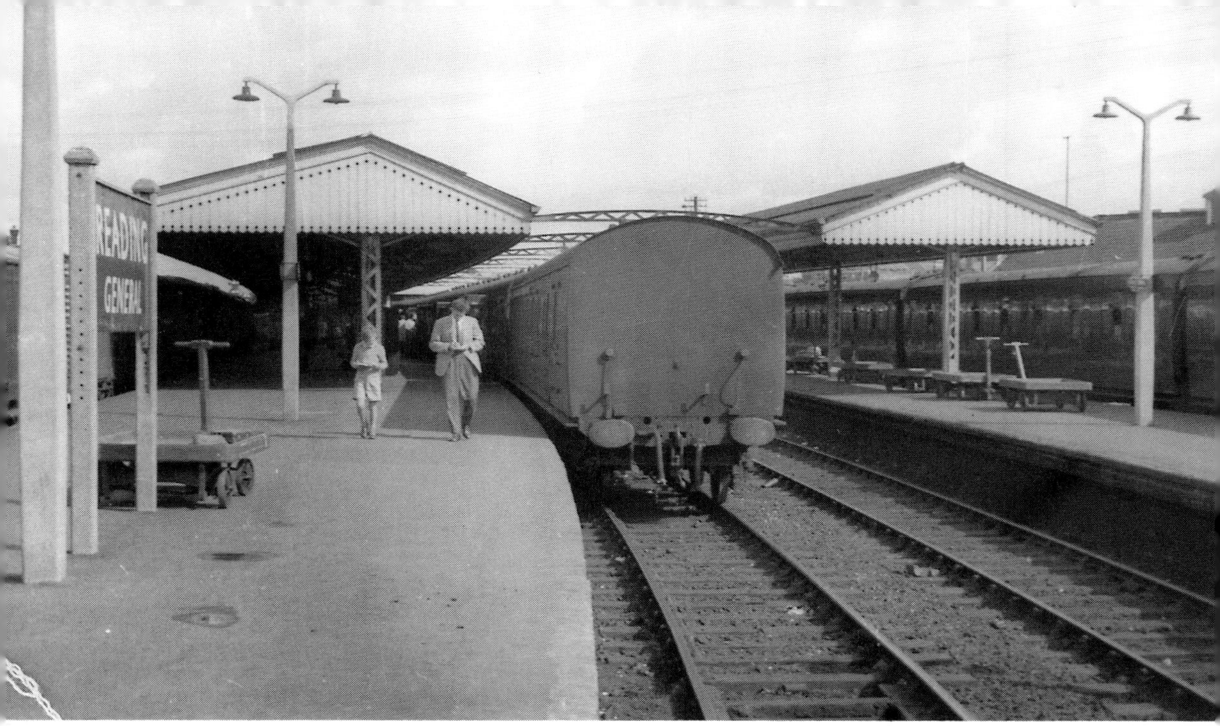
READING
GENERAL

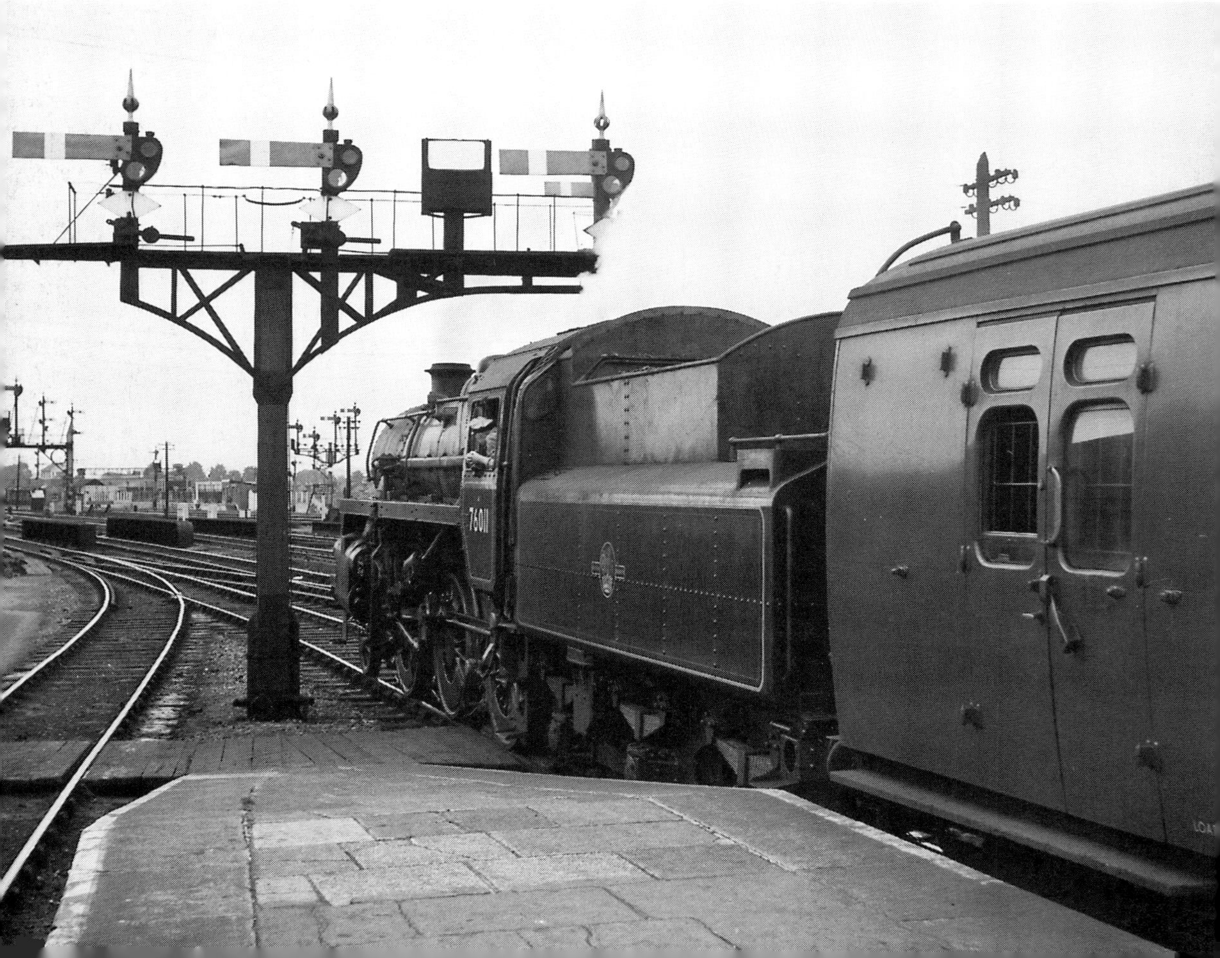
76011

9. While the canopy on platforms 1 and 2 is symmetrical, that on 3 and 4 is imbalanced. The girders between them presumably help to spread the resulting load on the stanchions. (Lens of Sutton)

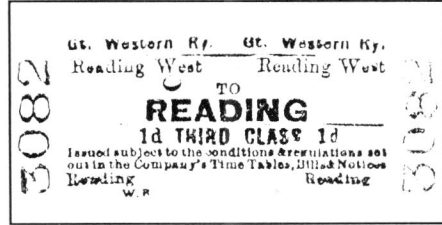

Gt. Western Ry.   Gt. Western Ry.
Reading West   Reading West
TO
READING
1d THIRD CLASS 1d
Issued subject to the conditions &regulations set out in the Company's Time Tables, Bills& Notices
Reading   Reading
W. R

10. An ex-SR Bulleid-designed coach forms part of the 11.55am to Portsmouth & Southsea on 4th August 1958, the BR Standard class 4 2-6-0 being no. 76011. On weekdays that summer there were two other departures to that station and two to Southampton Terminus, the remaining seven being to Basingstoke only. (M.Mensing)

11. The 16.00 departure for Portsmouth Harbour on Sunday 27th September 1981 was composed of no. 33117 hauling a 4TC set. These had a driving compartment at each end and were provided for the 1967 Bournemouth electrification scheme. (T.Heavyside)

12. An unusually clean Metropolitan Cammel DMU approaches platform 1 on 26th March 1988, havng worked a stopping service from Bedwyn, on the Newbury line. The roofscape was later totally transformed by office buildings. (P.G.Barnes)

13. Of the three types of diesel units seen on 2nd June 1990, only that nearest to the camera was to be found in regular use at Reading by December 1993. Class 165 units had replaced the others. (P.G.Barnes)

14. An eastward view on 8th August 1990 reveals the simplified junction arrangements. The single track nearest the house was used by local trains to and from Basingstoke. Diverging from it is a single berthing siding. (V.Mitchell)

15. Taken a few seconds after the previous picture, this features no. 47264 on a mail train at platform 3. Platform 10 was also used predominantly for this traffic. The "modern" office block on the right was replaced by one with more style in 1993. (V.Mitchell)

16. The ubiquitous class 47 could be seen on a wide variety of traffic. No. 47347 runs through platform 5 on 30th November 1991 bound for Southampton Maritime Container Terminal. The apparent gap to the platform is explained in picture no. 6. The extension was to increase the length of platform 7. All the other lines through the station are signalled for reversible running. (P.G.Barnes)

17. At platform 1 on 4th April 1992 is the 16.10 to Newbury while at platform 2 is the 16.20 to Basingstoke. This is worked by a class 205 DEMU, originally classified 3H when built as 3-car units for use in Hampshire. (P.G.Barnes)

18. The class 205 DEMUs were replaced by quieter and lighter class 165 Turbo diesels in May 1993 on the Basingstoke route. They were introduced to the Redhill and Gatwick Airport services in the following November. HSTs stand at platforms 4 and 5 on 3rd August 1993, the date also for the next two photographs. (V.Mitchell)

19. King Edward VII gazes at the new station complex which was completed in 1989, his great granddaughter, Queen Elizabeth II, opening the Brunel Arcade of shops therein on 4th April. Above the King's crown is the window cleaning gantry. Heathrow Railair Link coaches wait beyond the right of the picture. (V.Mitchell)

20. The spacious interior has a complex roof structure which requires the minimum number of supports. There is also a pair of escalators on platforms 5/8 and the footbridge (evident in picture 16) is pleasant to use being fully glazed, unlike the gloomy box provided at London Bridge station. (V.Mitchell)

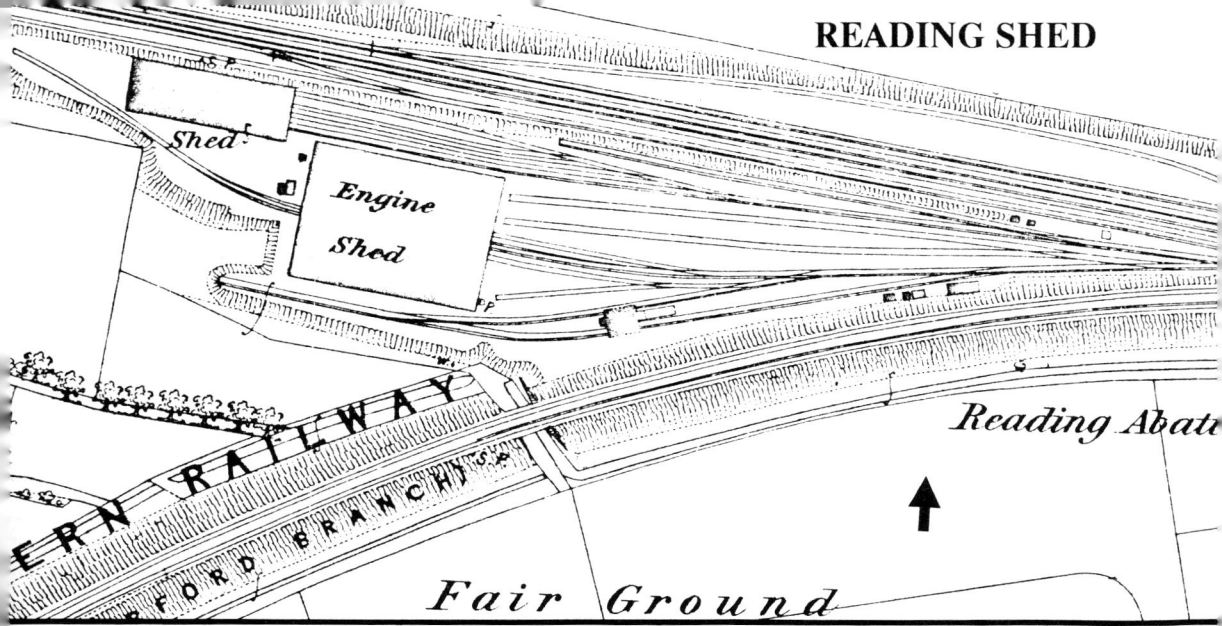

Shed

Engine Shed

ERN RAILWAY

FORD BRANCH

Reading Abat

Fair Ground

The 1879 map includes the engine shed that was opened in the following year within the triangular junction. It replaced the 1840 shed which was north of the station, on a site later developed for goods traffic. Broad, standard and mixed gauge tracks can be distinguished. The line to Basingstoke (lower left) is shown as broad although records suggest that this section was mixed from 1858.

21. This photograph dates from about 1921 and includes no. 3810 *County Wicklow* (left), no. 3407 *Madras* (centre) and no. 3386 *Paddingdon* (right). The shed contained a central 45ft. turntable, with 20 lines radiating from it. These were replaced by nine straight tracks in about 1930, following the provision of a 65ft. turntable in the shed yard in 1925. (G.W.Trust)

22. This 1947 westward view includes the Basingstoke and West of England line (left) and a GWR diesel railcar (right). A diesel multiple unit servicing depot in a three-road shed was completed behind the engine shed in August 1959. (M.W.Earley/National Railway Museum)

23. Steam still reigned supreme, albeit grimy, when the yard was recorded in August 1950. In the foreground is 6100 class no. 6105, a type introduced in 1931. The shed had seven more of this class, 15 class 4300 2-6-0s, 19 class 5700 0-6-0Ts, 19 "Halls", 2 "Castles", 3 "Granges", 20 other locomotives and 4 railcars.
(Wessex coll.)

24. The depot's coaling and ash disposal steam crane was photographed in August 1950 along with a string of pannier tanks and one of the water sources. The last steam working from the shed took place on 2nd January 1965. The final scheduled steam hauled train through Reading was the 9.18am from Paddington to Bristol and Gloucester on 27th November 1965, headed by no. 7029 *Clun Castle*.
(Wessex coll.)

25. The DMU servicing shed was extended in 1964 to allow for the maintenance of diesel locomotives. On 1st June 1985 an open day was held at the depot and a variety of rolling stock from other areas was on show. This was one of the last duties for no. 25302. (M.J.Stretton)

26. On the same day, some civil engineering equipment was on display, the Wickham inspection car causing some amusement. The permanent way school moved to the site of the steam shed in 1985. (M.J.Stretton)

27. The PW depot at Theale closed in 1972 and was moved to the site on the right of this picture, which was taken from a train bound for Basingstoke on 27th April 1991. The diesel depot had been further enlarged by the addition of a new two-track building in 1981. Owing to the new trains being 18ft. longer than their predecessors, the offices at the end of the shed were lost in 1992. New ones were built at the rear. (R.E.Ruffell)

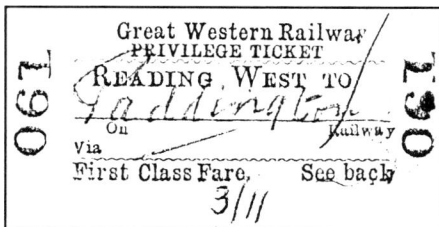

Great Western Railway
PRIVILEGE TICKET
READING WEST TO
Paddington
On   Railway
Via
First Class Fare,   See back
3/11
060   060

28. New refuelling facilities were provided in 1987 and this new building for "traincare services" followed in 1991. Alongside is the washing plant and, out of view, is the toilet reception tank emptying facility. (M.Turvey)

SOUTH OF READING

29. Passing between the locomotive depot and the carriage sidings in 1947 is no. 6010 *King Charles I* with a train from the West of England. In that year of austerity there were no expresses shown on the Basingstoke route in the December timetable. Semaphore signalling ceased in the Reading area in 1965. (M.W.Earley/National Railway Museum)

30. A view south across the civil engineer's crane test area in August 1990 includes a DEMU departing for Basingstoke, while another from that town waits at the signal to use the single line section to platform 2. (V.Mitchell)

32. A February 1993 view from the same spot on Reading West up platform includes the 1938 steel girders and the 1991 Turbo depot with one such unit at the end of the siding. (M.J.Stretton)

31. Oxford Road Junction is at the southern apex of the triangular junction and is seen before the rebuilding of the bridge in 1938. At that time the points were moved to the other end of the bridge. (Dr P.Ransome-Wallis/ National Railway Museum)

READING WEST

33. The station was opened on 1st July 1906 and was provided with long platforms to accommodate trains running between the South Coast and the Midlands. By stopping here, instead of the main station, they were able to avoid a reversal and change of locomotive. The down platform was later extended to accommodate trains clear of the junction. (Lens of Sutton)

Reading West	1913	1923	1933
Passenger tickets issued	22050	60430	36995
Season tickets issued	56	312	308
Parcels forwarded	4729	5646	4731

34.   The platforms were of wooden construction to minimise the weight on the embankment. Despite this consideration, cast iron posts were used for the gas lights.
(Lens of Sutton)

35.   The signal is off for the train to take the Reading avoiding line from Oxford Road Junction to Reading West Junction, known as Reading West curve. The low sun on 12th January 1929 has not melted all the frost on the sleepers and gives a dramatic backlight on the locomotive, Dean Goods class 2301 no. 2479.
(H.C.Casserley)

36. No. 6028 *King George VI* passes over Oxford Road brick arch shortly before its demolition in 1938. The notice on the arch *KEEP YOUR SEATS* was directed at upper deck tram passengers. Just visible is the overhead wire of the tramway that was in use from 1903 until 1939. (M.W.Earley/National Railway Museum)

G. W. RLY. S,3

The holder is prohibited from entering the Company's trains

Not Transferable 1 D.

Admit ONE to PLATFORM

Available ONE HOUR on DAY of ISSUE ONLY,

This Ticket must be given up on leaving Platform.

FOR CONDITIONS SEE BACK,

READING WEST

804   804

1 | 2 | 3 | 4 | 5 | 6

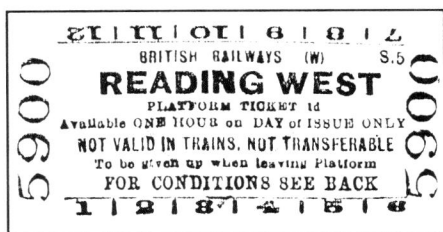

37. Single line working was in operation during the bridge replacement, the event attracting the attention of passing passengers and local youth alike. The locomotive, semi-streamlined *King Henry VII*, is regaining the down road. Only one other locomotive was fitted with this experimental feature, that being no. 5005 *Manorbier Castle*.
(M.W.Earley/National Railway Museum)

38. Working a Portsmouth & Southsea train on 16th April 1953 is class H15 no. 30474. By this time much of the platform had been reconstructed with concrete slabs. Both the locomotive and the coaches were of LSWR design, although the former was not built until 1924. (V.Webster)

39. August 1963 and no. 34084 *253 Squadron* hauls a train off the Reading West curve. The leading coach is from the Eastern Region so this may be one of the trains that originated at Newcastle. (H.F.Wheeller)

```
        2nd-SINGLE SINGLE-2nd
  (M)        Reading West to         (M)
        Reading West      Reading West
        Reading General   Reading General
  [N]      READING GENERAL           [N]
  (O)  (W)  3d   FARE   3d  (W)      (O)
       For conditions see over  For conditions see over
```

40. The DEMUs received warning triangles to make them more obvious to track workers sometime after this photograph was taken in April 1966. Between the rails on the left is one of the ramps for the GWR's automatic warning system. (C.L.Caddy)

41. Hymek no. D7057 creeps into the station with a parcels train on 11th August 1966, probably on a shunting move as an oil tail lamp is on the front. These locomotives became class 35 in the 1970s. (J.H.Bird)

42. Pictures 32 and 33 were taken from the platform ramp on the right. This 1993 picture shows Network SouthEast markings but the birds appear to be InterCity swifts suffering collision damage. (M.J.Stretton)

43. For its final period in service no. 205029 was repainted in its original green livery, but high visibility ends were retained. The yellow band above the doors indicates that there were only two first class compartments. The date is 10th February 1993. (M.J.Stretton)

44. On 24th February 1993 no. 165135 was working the 11.00 from Newbury while no. 207017 departs as the 11.18 Reading to Basingstoke. The new coaches have internal dot matrix displays indicating the stations served. The destination is shown on the ends. (M.Turvey)

45. In pristine condition, class X2 no. E590 makes a fine sight as it runs south in the early days of the Southern Railway. The entire train is of LSWR origin, and was recorded after 1925 when the locomotive was repainted. (H.J.Patterson Rutherford)

46. Another photograph from the late 1920s features a very unusual engine for the route. It is ex-SECR class R1 no. 1709 which had probably been borrowed from the SR shed at Reading. Look at the crisp shadow. (H.J.Patterson Rutherford)

47. The line required a deep cutting to pass through the headland between the Thames and Kennet valleys. No. 59002 *Yeoman Enterprise* is passing through it with a long empty stone train. It is bound for Merehead Quarry in Somerset on 13th July 1990. (J.S.Petley)

2nd - SINGLE   SINGLE - 2nd

1243

Reading West to

Reading West
Reading General

Reading West
Reading General

READING GENERAL

(W)   4d. Fare 4d.   (W)

For conditions see over   For conditions see over

1243

S.P.

WINSER DRIVE

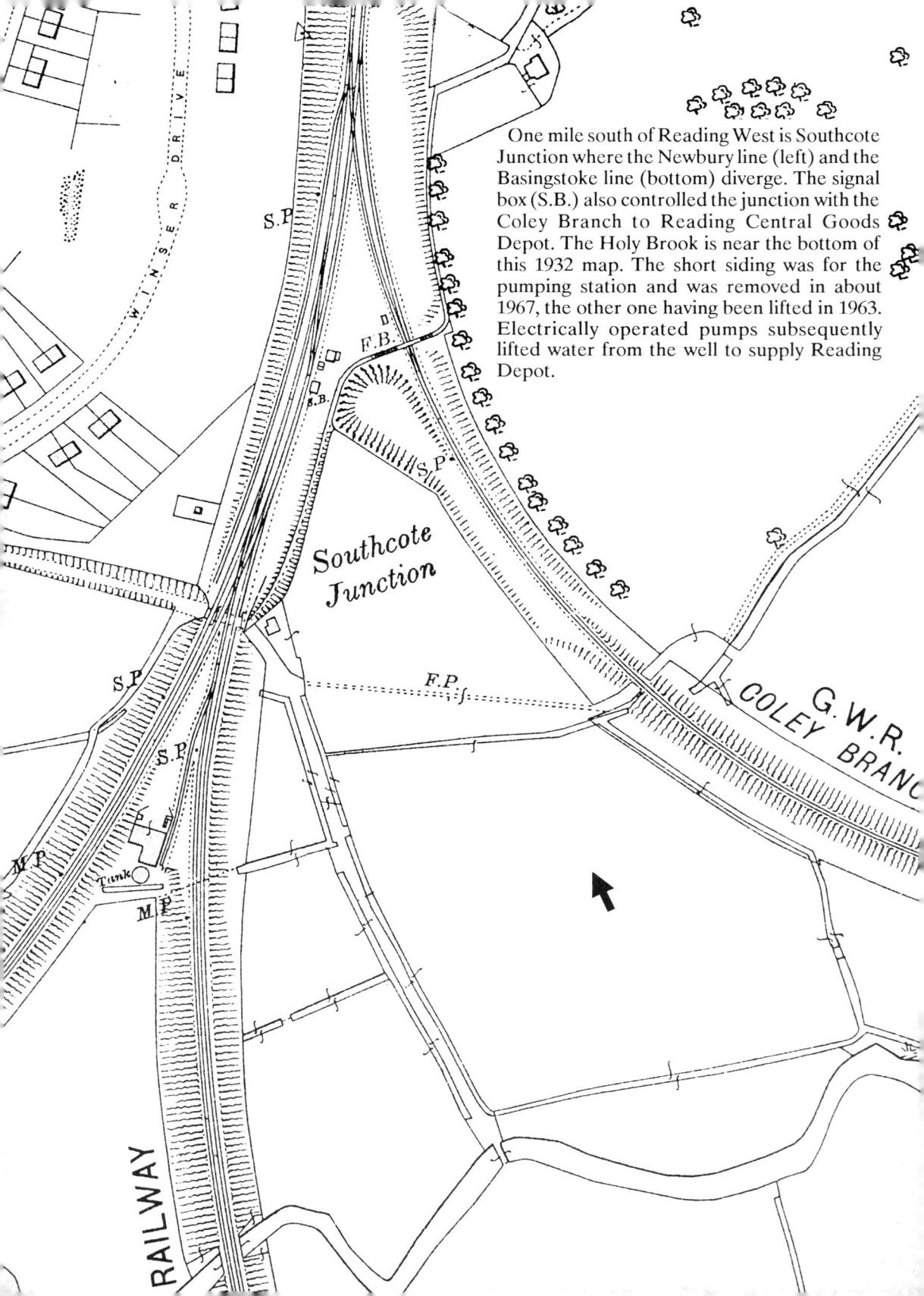

One mile south of Reading West is Southcote Junction where the Newbury line (left) and the Basingstoke line (bottom) diverge. The signal box (S.B.) also controlled the junction with the Coley Branch to Reading Central Goods Depot. The Holy Brook is near the bottom of this 1932 map. The short siding was for the pumping station and was removed in about 1967, the other one having been lifted in 1963. Electrically operated pumps subsequently lifted water from the well to supply Reading Depot.

F.B.

S.B.

S.P.

Southcote
Junction

S.P.

F.P.

S.P.

S.P.

G.W.R.
COLEY BRANCH

M.P.

Tank

M.P.

RAILWAY

48. The Coley Branch is on the left and Southcote Junction box is in the distance as class 2251 no. 3219 plods north with its train of tankers in 1955. The box closed on 25th April 1965, Reading Panel taking over control of the junction. (M.W.Earley/National Railway Museum.)

49. Eleven years before this photograph was taken, on 5th February 1967, the Coley Branch had been singled and the signal box had gone. The train is the LCGB "South West Suburban Railtour" which is returning from Reading Central Goods behind class 4 2-6-0 no. 76058. (J.H.Bird)

COLEY BRANCH

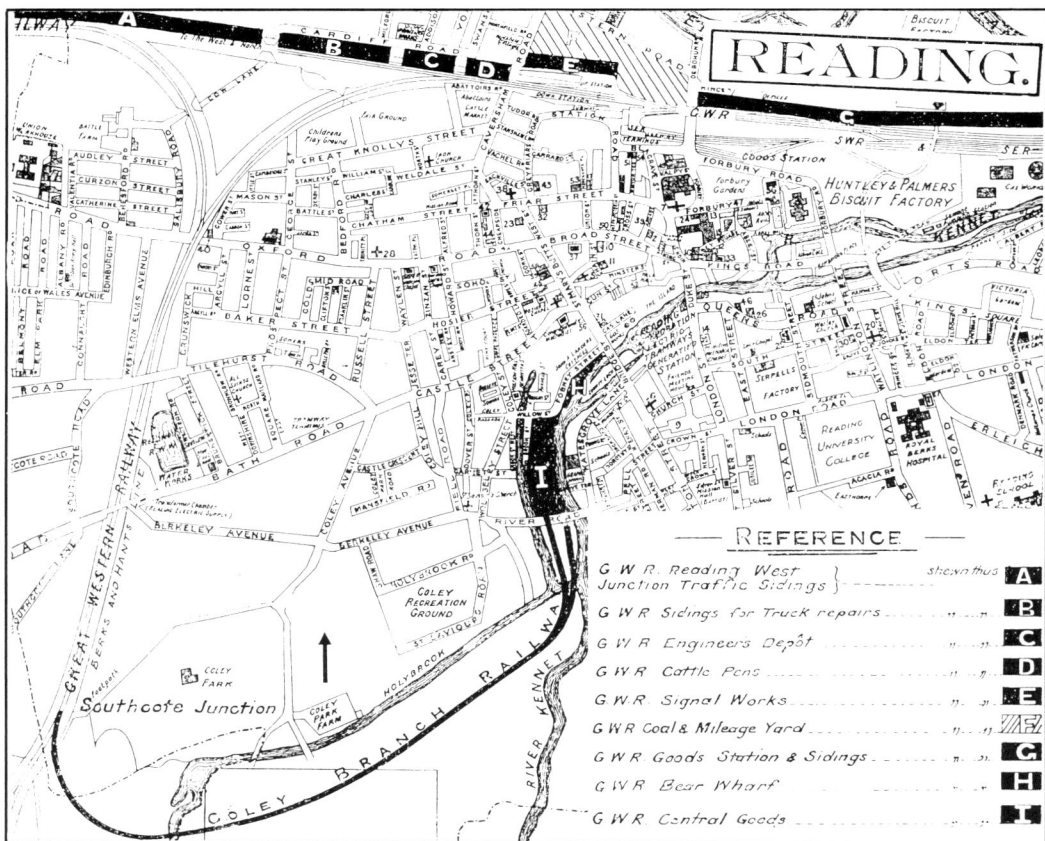

This unscaled map was reproduced in the GWR Magazine in June 1908 to indicate the position of the branch and the new Central Goods Depot which had opened on May 4th of that year. It had become necessary owing to congestion in the existing yards and the problems of carting goods through the busy town centre.

The REFERENCE on the map lists:

Reference		
G.W.R. Reading West Junction Traffic Sidings	shown thus	**A**
G.W.R. Sidings for Truck repairs	,, ,,	**B**
G.W.R. Engineers Depot	,, ,,	**C**
G.W.R. Cattle Pens	,, ,,	**D**
G.W.R. Signal Works	,, ,,	**E**
G.W.R. Coal & Mileage Yard	,, ,,	**F**
G.W.R. Goods Station & Sidings	,, ,,	**G**
G.W.R. Bear Wharf	,, ,,	**H**
G.W.R. Central Goods	,, ,,	**I**

The GWR offered favourable terms to industrial organisations for sidings alongside new factories. Two tracks pass through gates to the sidings of the Co-operative jam factory. This is the 1932 survey.

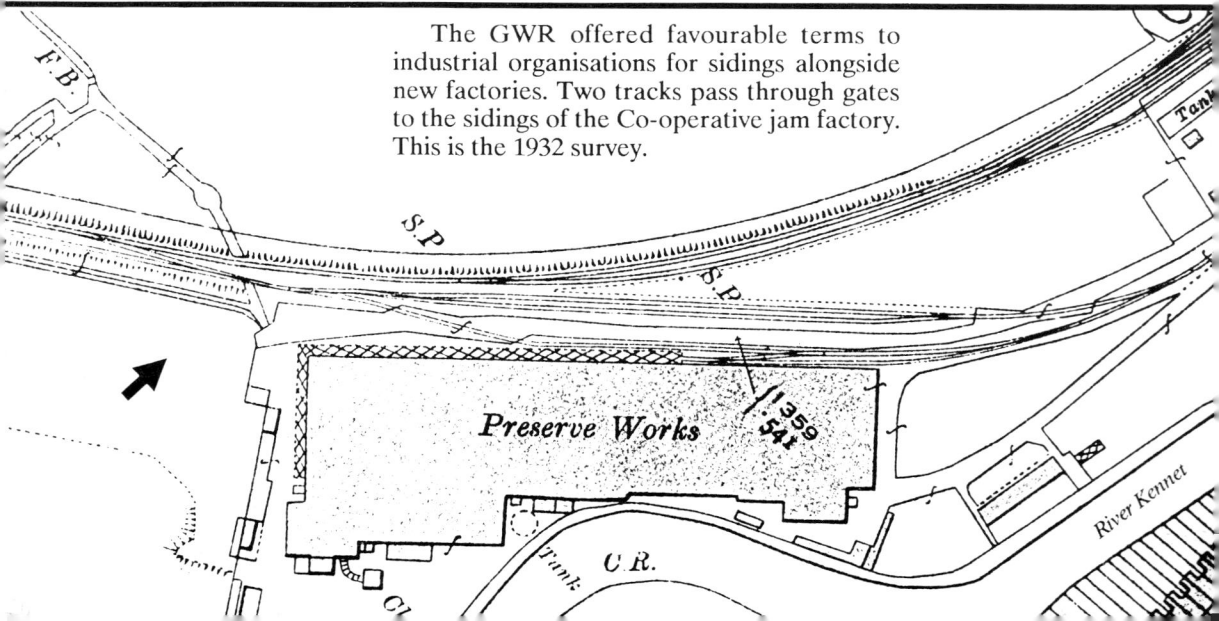

COLEY STREET

Fn.

BOSIER'S SQUARE

Hall

F.B.

Workmen's Hall

PARNELL ST.

BRIGHT STREET

Malthouse

FOBN

F.B.

Sls.

M Ps

County Lock

M.Ps

Tannery

130

HENRIETTA ST.

WILLOW STREET

Beer Wharf

Mooring Posts

KATESGROVE LANE

FOUNDRY

COLEY PLACE

P.H.

P.H.

BROOK STREET WEST

BROOK STREET

W.M.

Cr.

TEMPLE PLACE

School

DOVER STREET

WOLSELEY STREET

School

HIGH

Brook

LOWER BROOK STREET

M.P

Printing Works

M.P

Central Goods Depôt (G.W.R.)

Printing Works

KATESGROVE TERRACE

135

School

COLEY

Allotment Gardens

River Kennet

RIVER ROAD

L.B.

St. Saviour's Church

Hall

Cr.

BERKELEY AVENUE

Saw Mill

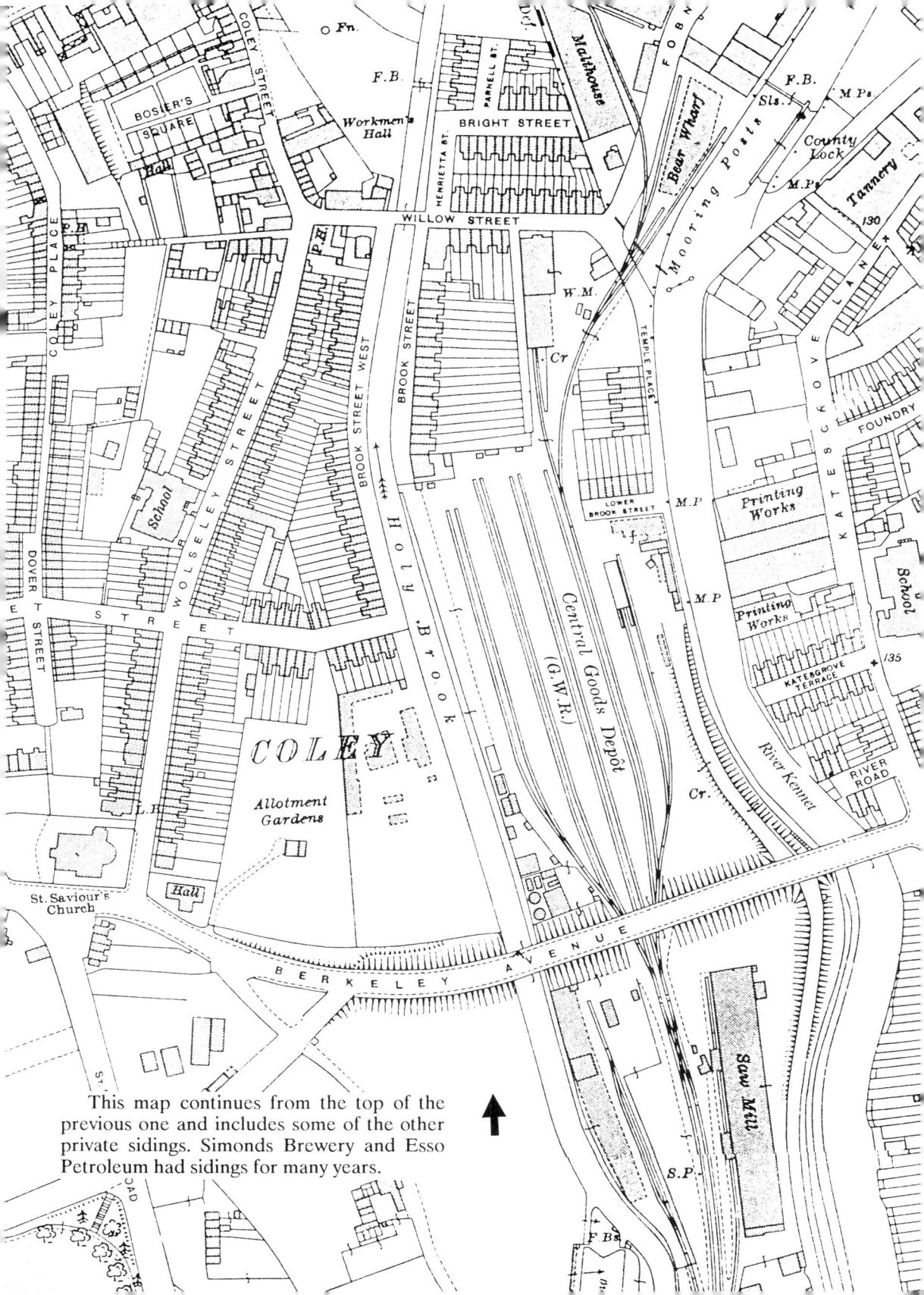

This map continues from the top of the previous one and includes some of the other private sidings. Simonds Brewery and Esso Petroleum had sidings for many years.

S.P.

F.Bs

50.   Central Goods Depot was officially recorded soon after opening in 1908. On the left are the stacks of half round timber sleepers and flat bottom rails from the temporary way of the contractors, Messrs. H. Lovatt & Co. of Wolverhampton. Most of the land had belonged to the Kennet & Avon Canal Company which had been purchased by the GWR in 1852. When opened the yard could accommodate 300 wagons, had a 20-ton cart weighbridge and a 10-ton crane, marked Cr. on the map. A horse enjoys its nosebag near the steamroller, while the workmen rest against a lamp post. (British Rail)

51. The single cottage with hipped roof is all that remains of the terrace seen in the previous picture. The other dwellings were demolished so that tracks could be laid to the goods shed and Bear Wharf. Also the three middle pairs of sidings were extended, as shown on the map. On the right is a traction engine and trailer. (G.W.Trust) ←——————

52. Ex-LSWR class M7 0-4-4T no. 30051 was in charge of the "Compass Rose" railtour on 3rd October 1957 which was composed of an LBSCR push-pull set. Tank engines had usually worked the goods traffic but they were invariably of GWR origin. Six such engines (commonly the 5700 class) were working round the clock in and between the various yards in Reading, one visiting this depot three or four times each day at its zenith. (N.C.Simmons)

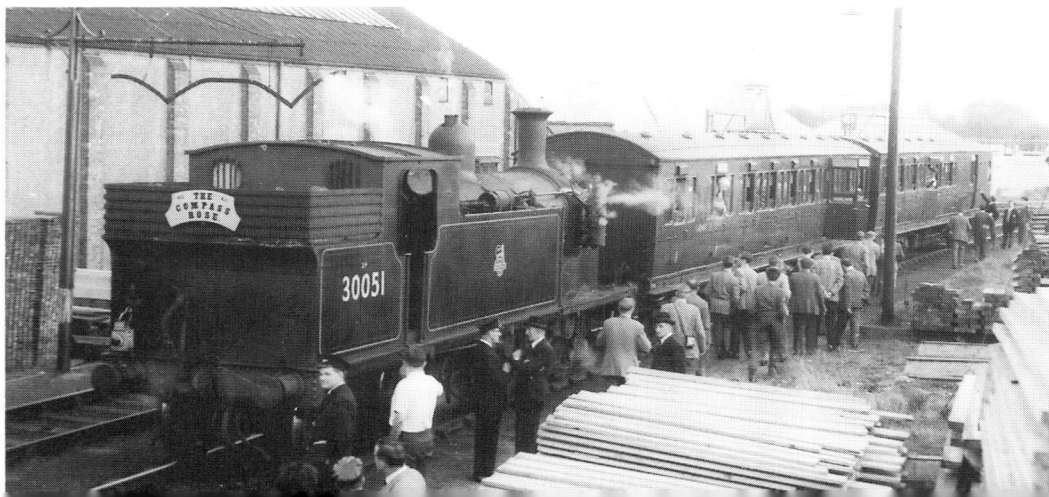

53.   The "South Western Suburban Rail Tour" was the 100th to be operated by the LCGB and ran on 5th February 1967. The branch was double track until 26th May 1956 and was capable of carrying all but the heavy "King" class locomotives. This southward view from River Road bridge shows site redevelopment already commencing. (J.H.Bird)

54.   A few minutes after the last photograph was taken, no. 76058 was shot running round its train. The goods shed and Bear Wharf closed on 20th March 1969 and complete closure followed on 25th July 1983. The branch was lifted in January 1985 but the footbridge near the junction still remained in 1994. (R.E.Ruffell)

Reading (All GWR depots)	1903	1913	1923	1933
General goods forwarded (tons)	82186	69055	41279	34325
Coal and coke received	217107	106871	95334	126137
Other minerals received	26126	11678	26021	32349
General goods received	123178	100039	89101	118528
Trucks of livestock handled	3363	3782	2402	2813

June - September 1962
Sunday trains are shown opposite
pictures 65 and 66.

Miles	Down		Mondays to Fridays																				
			am T	am	am T	am T	am		am R	am T	am T	am	pm	pm T	pm W	pm T		pm L	pm	pm T	pm Z	pm T
—	**Reading General** ... ... dep		6 35	6 50	7 15	7 53	8 53	...	9 53	1053	1153	1230	1 5	...	1 53	...	2 53	3 21	3 53	...	5 0
¾	Reading West .... ,,		6 39	6 55	7 19	7 57	8 57	...	9 56	1057	1157	1234	9	1 45	1 57	...	2 57	3 25	3 57	4 6	5 4
7¼	Mortimer . .. — — — ,,		6 48	7 6	7 28	8 6	9 6	...	10 5	11 6	12 6	1243	18	...	2 6	...	3 6	3 34	4 6	...	5 13
10½	Bramley .... ,,		6 54	7 15	7 34	8 12	9 12	...	10 11	1112	1212	1249	24	...	2 12	...	3 12	3 40	4 12	...	5 19
15½	**Basingstoke.. .. .. .. arr**		7 2	7 26	7 42	8 20	9 22	...	10 19	1122	1220	1257	32	2	9	2 20	...	3 20	3 48	4 20	4 36	5 28
51¼	**35** Salisbury .... arr		...	8 46	...	10 3	1050	...	11 56	1 26		2 22	...	...	3 57	...	...	4 41	5 57	...	...
62¾	**32, 54** Portsmouth & Southsea ,,		...	9 18	...	9 49	1041	...	11 35	1235	1 41	...	2 47	...	3 35	...	4 35	...	5 35	6 14	6 43
46¾	**32** Southampton Terminus ,,		...	3 45	...	9 6	1013	...	...	1215	11	...	2 24	...	3 11	...	...	5 10	...	6 19
47	**32** ,, Central . ,,		...	3 49	...	...	1023	...	11 25	1233	12	...	2 33	3	13	14	...	4 19	...	5 27	5 37	6 33
75¾	**32** Bournemouth Central . ,,		...	10 5	...	10 30	1114	...	12 21	...	2 23	...	...	3 59	4 15	...	5 40	...	6 26	6 37	...
79¼	**32** ,, West .. ,,		...	...	...	10 42	1131	...	12 33	...	2 37	...	...	4 11	4 33	...	5 57	...	6 40	6 50	...

Down		Mondays to Fridays—continued									Saturdays										
		pm	pm T	pm	pm T	pm T	pm T	pm	pm X	pm	pm		am	am T	am T	am R	am H	am T	am N	am T	am Y	pm	pm T
Reading General ... ... dep		5 14	5 48	7 0	7 53	8 53	9 21	9 53	11 2	...	6 35	6 50	7 53	9 7	9 53	1050	...	1153	...	...	1230	1 5
Reading West .... ,,		5 18	5 52	7 4	7 57	8 57	9 25	9 57	...	6 39	6 55	7 57	9 10	9 56	...	11 3	1157	1219	1234	1 9
Mortimer . .. — — — ,,		5 27	6 1	7 13	8 6	9 6	9 34	10 6	11 13	...	6 48	7 6	8 6	9 20	10 5	11 2	...	12 6	...	1243	1 18
Bramley .... ,,		5 33	6 7	7 19	8 12	9 12	9 40	10 12	11 19	...	6 54	7 15	8 12	9 27	10 11	11 9	...	1212	...	1249	1 24
Basingstoke.. .. .. .. arr		5 41	6 17	7 30	8 20	9 20	9 48	10 20	11 31	...	7 2	7 26	8 20	9 35	10 19	11 20	1131	1220	1244	1257	1 32
35 Salisbury .... arr		7 0	7 45	...	9 41	...	...	11 36	2e27	...	8 46	9 42	10 50	...	1 15	1 15	...	...	...	2 22	...
32, 54 Portsmouth & Southsea ,,		...	7 35	8 47	9 1036	...	11 54	2o28	...	9 21	9 47	10 50	11 36	1250	1 51	2 18	...	2 47
32 Southampton Terminus ,,		...	7 11	8 19	9 11	1011	...	12o54	...	8 44	9 6	10 27	11 15	1218	...	1 14	...	2 23
32 ,, Central . ,,		...	7 19	8 33	9 25	...	11 9	...	...	8 49	9 34	10e29	11 27	1233	1256	1 21	...	2 33
32 Bournemouth Central . ,,		...	8 17	9f51	1013	...	12n 5	2o11	...	10 7	10k24	11 58	12 27	1 35	1 54	2 23	...	3 50
32 ,, West .. ,,		...	8 29	...	1027	...	...	...	...	...	10k36	...	...	1 47	...	2 37	...	...

Down		Saturdays—continued																			
		pm R	pm T		pm J	pm	pm T	pm K	pm Z		pm Q	pm		pm T	pm T		pm T	pm T		pm	pm X	pm
Reading General ... ... dep		1 53	2 53	.	...	3 21	3 53	...	...	...	5 0	5 18	...	5 53	7 0	...	7 53	8 53	...	9 21	9 53	11 2
Reading West .... ,,		1 57	2 57	3	5	3 25	3 57	4	2 4 32	...	5 4	5 22	...	5 57	7 4	...	7 57	8 57	...	9 25	9 57	...
Mortimer . .. — — — ,,		2 6	3 6	.	...	3 34	4 6	...	...	...	5 13	5 31	...	6 6	7 13	...	8 6	9 8	...	9 34	10 6	11 13
Bramley .... ,,		2 12	3 12	.	...	3 40	4 12	...	...	...	5 19	5 37	...	6 12	7 19	...	8 12	9 14	...	9 40	1012	11 19
Basingstoke.. .. .. .. arr		2 20	3 20	.	3 27	3 48	4 20	4 36	4 55	...	5 28	5 45	...	6 20	7 30	...	8 20	9 20	...	9 48	1020	11 30
35 Salisbury .... arr		3 56	...	...	...	4 41	5 57	...	...	...	7 0	...	7 45	...	...	9 41	...	...	113r	2h27
32, 54 Portsmouth & Southsea ,,		3 35	4 41	...	...	5 35	6 14	...	6 43	...	7 35	8 47	9 35	1036	...	1154	2b28
32 Southampton Terminus ,,		3 17	4 15	...	...	5 10	...	6 21	...	7 11	8 19	9 11	1012	...	...	12b54
32 ,, Central . ,,		3 19	4 28	.	4 28	...	5 26	5 37	6 11	...	6 33	...	7 19	8 33	...	9 25	...	...	11 5	1b 9
32 Bournemouth Central . ,,		4 20	5 31	.	5 31	...	6 26	40	7 16	...	...	8 17	...	...	1013	...	...	12n9	2b 2
32 ,, West .. ,,		4 38	...	...	...	6 40	...	7 28	...	...	8 29	...	...	1027	...	...	...	...

H Through Train Reading General to Portsmouth Harbour arr 11 40 am
J Restaurant Car Train Birkenhead Woodside to Bournemouth Central (Table 15)
K Through Train Bradford Exchange to Poole (Table 16)
L Through Train Reading General to Portsmouth and Southsea; also to Southampton Central
N Through Train Birmingham (Moor St.) to Portsmouth and Southsea 14th July to 18th August
Q Through Train Reading General to Portsmouth and Southsea; also to Southampton Terminus

R Through Train Reading General to Portsmouth & Southsea
T Through Train Reading General to Southampton Terminus
W Restaurant Car Train Wolverhampton (Low Level) to Bournemouth West (Table 15)
X Through Train Reading General to Eastleigh (arr 10 56 pm) (Table 32)
Y Through Train Birmingham (Snow Hill) to Portsmouth Harbour arr 2 23 pm
Z Restaurant Car Train Newcastle Central to Bournemouth West (Table 16)

a am
b am. Sunday mornings
e am. Via Eastleigh. On Thursday mornings only arr 1 27 am
f Fridays only commencing 6th July
h Sunday mornings via Eastleigh
k Applies until 25th August
n Midnight
q Applies until 1st September

MORTIMER

55. The station opened with the line and was initially the only intermediate one. Note the beautifuly designed garden, the road transport and that the rails are on longitudinal timbers with tie bars. This had been Brunel's specification for the broad gauge tracks. (Lens of Sutton)

56. The legacy of the broad gauge era is the wide space between the tracks, normally known as the "six-foot". The signal is remote from the line it relates to, owing to the curve. The local population was 1270 in 1901, increasing to 1577 fifty years later. (Lens of Sutton)

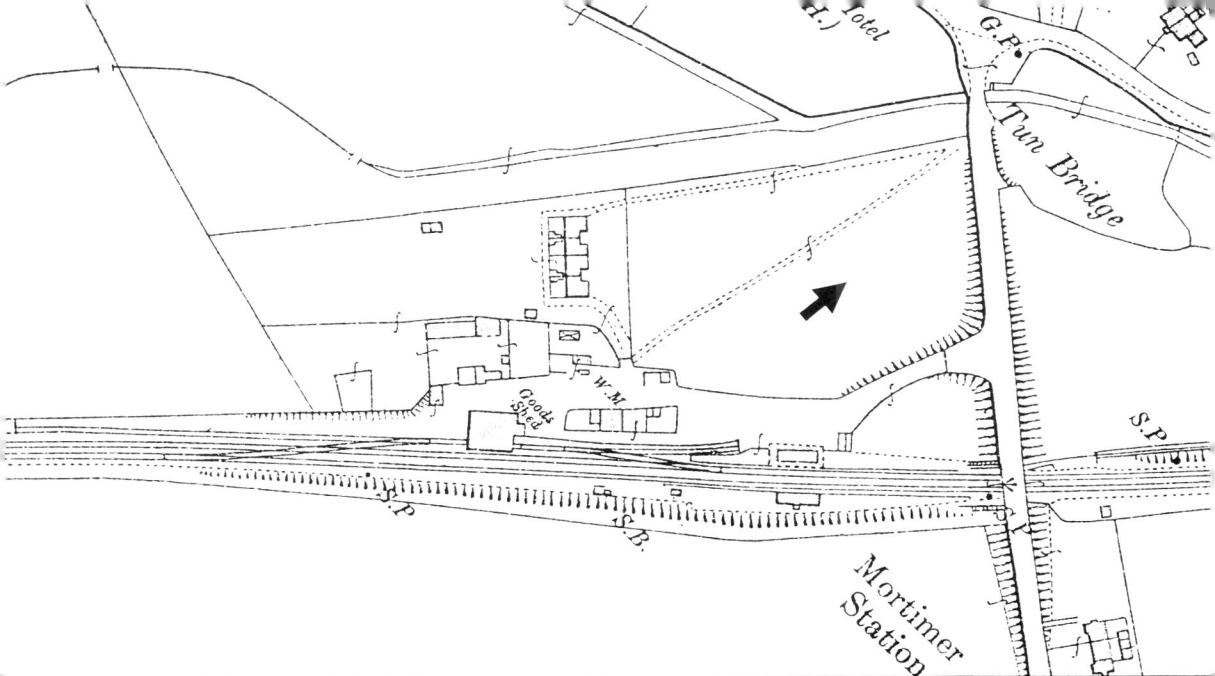

The 1911 survey shows an arrangement that changed little until the closure of the goods yard on 6th March 1963.

57. While the main line has bullhead rail, the siding retains its bridge rail, a type that was used on broad gauge track. Hay was a dangerous commodity to transport - a wagonload from Pluckley (Kent) was destroyed in Reading on 4th April 1946 due to a spark from a shunting engine. (Lens of Sutton)

Mortimer	1903	1913	1923	1933
Passenger tickets issued	32483	31278	31757	19940
Season tickets issued	-	113	395	153
Parcels forwarded	16075	21795	22196	6675
General goods forwarded (tons)	1110	1084	727	448
Coal and coke received	8643	6298	6195	4896
Other minerals received	1810	1829	2432	3238
General goods received	2021	2223	1371	431
Trucks of livestock handled	82	132	124	15

Burghfield Factory

This was established in about 1940 by the War Department and passed to the Ministry of Supply. It was administered by the Ministry of Defence from 1964, the factory having become an Atomic Weapons Research Establishment. Three 0-4-0STs were supplied new in 1941, an 0-4-0DM following in 1946. The three steam locomotives were transferred to ROF Rotherwas near Hereford in 1957, when the rail system closed. Owing to security restrictions, no photographs are available. A low curved embankment was still visible on the west side of the main line in 1994.

58.   A Morris 8 and a Standard 10 grace the yard as BR Standard class 4 4-6-0 no. 75077 works a train to Southampton on 13th August 1960. The white patch on the track suggests that there has been a pumping action from loose sleepers. The heap of stones will help to remedy the problem. (T.Wright)

59. A southward view on 2nd April 1966 reveals that the sidings have gone, as has the roof of the footbridge. The signal box had closed on 28th June 1964. Another was in use three miles north of the station from 22nd June 1941 to 10th February 1963 controlling double track access to Burghfield depot, west of the route. Further north, a down goods loop at Pound Green was operational from 1940 to 1950. (C.L.Caddy)

60. Full time staffing ceased on 5th October 1969 but this 1988 photo confirms that the structure had been well maintained subsequently. In its latter years the signal box had been manned only on summer Saturdays. (J.Scrace)

61. After the hustle and bustle of Reading, Mortimer presents a tranquil atmosphere, particularly after the passing of the throbbing engine of no. 207005. It is working the 13.55 Reading to Portsmouth Harbour on 30th September 1988. (J.Scrace)

62. The 12.05 from Basingstoke (no. 207010) has stopped on 7th April 1993 as the 12.03 from Reading (no. 43067) speeds south. This HST had started at Manchester Piccadilly at 08.18 and was due at Bournemouth at 13.40. The architectural style was a link with the Brunel era. (T.Wright)

63. DEMU no. 205029 passes under the new footbridge, erected in September 1992. It is forming the 12.48 Reading to Basingstoke, a service which by that time had become half-hourly. The addition of a headlight had improved trackside visibility of these units. (M.J.Stretton)

64. Speeding near Mortimer on 11th April 1987 is no. 47410 with the 09.02 Manchester Piccadilly to Poole. This service was cut back to terminate at Bournemouth upon the introduction of HSTs. (A.Dasi-Sutton)

Down — Sundays

		am K		am N		am R		am K		am K		pm K		pm K		pm K	pm K
Reading General	.. dep	7 53	..	8 53	..	9 53	..	1053	..	1153	..	1253	..	1 53	..	2 53
Reading West	,,	7 57	..	8 57	..	9 57	..	1057	..							2 57
Mortimer	,,	8 6	..	9 6	..	10 6	..	11 8	..	12 6	..	1 6	..	2 6	..	3 6
Bramley	,,	8 12	..	9 12	..	1012	..	1114	..	1212	..	1 12	..	2 12	..	3 12
Basingstoke	arr	8 20	..	9 20	..	1022	..	1122	..	1220	..	1 20	..	2 20	..	3 20
35 Salisbury	arr			1050		1155		1247								
32,54 Portsmouth & Southsea	,,	9 35	..	1035	..	1135	..	1235	..	1 41	..	2 42	..	3 47	..	4 35
32 Southampton Terminus	,,															
32 ,, Central	,,	9 11	..	1024	..	1113	..	1218	..	1 7	..	2 15	..	3 21	..	4 11
32 Bournemouth Central	,,			1122		1222		1 42		2 8				4 7		
32 ,, West	,,			1139		1234				2 20				4 24		

Down — Sundays—continued

		pm K		pm K		pm K		pm K		pm K		pm		pm K		pm X		pm R		pm		pm Z
Reading General	.. dep	3 53	..	4 53	..	5 53	..	6 53	..	7 53	..	8 35	..	8 53	..	9 53	..	1015	..	10 53
Reading West	,,	3 57	..	4 57	..	5 57	..	6 57	..	7 57	..	8 39	..	8 57	..	9 57	..	1019	..	
Mortimer	,,	4 6	..	5 6	..	6 6	..	7 6	..	8 6	..	8 48	..	9 6	..	10 6	..	1028	..	11 4
Bramley	,,	4 12	..	5 12	..	6 12	..	7 12	..	8 12	..	8 54	..	9 12	..	1012	..	1034	..	11 10
Basingstoke	arr	4 20	..	5 22	..	6 20	..	7 20	..	8 22	..	9 2	..	9 20	..	1020	..	1042	..	11 18
35 Salisbury	arr	5 46	..			7 42	..			9 35	..	10 0	..					1155	..	2d27
32,54 Portsmouth & Southsea	,,	5 35	..	6 35	..	7 35	..	8 35	..	9 35	..			1042	..			1158	..	2d28
32 Southampton Terminus	,,																			12d59
32 ,, Central	,,	5 11	..	6 15	..	7 11	..	8 11	..	9 13	..			1011	..	1121	..			
32 Bournemouth Central	,,	6 25	..			8 44	..	9 24	..					1058	..					2 d12
32 ,, West	,,					9 3	..	9 38	..					1110						

Up — Sundays

		am K		am V		am K		am K		am K		am K		pm K		pm K
32 Bournemouth West	.. dep							9 25	..	1026	..	1056	..			
32 ,, Central	,,							9 36	..	1036	..	1116	..			
32 Southampton Central	,,	7 25	..	8 25	..	9 25	..	1025	..	1125	..	1225	..	1 25	..	2 25
32 ,, Terminus	,,															
32,54 Portsmouth & Southsea	,,	6 53	..	7 53	..	8 53	..	9 53	..	1053	..	1153	..	1253	..	1 53
35 Salisbury	,,					8 30	..	10 5	..							1 58
Basingstoke	dep	8 17	..	9 17	..	1017	..	1117	..	1217	..	1 17	..	2 17	..	3 17
Bramley	,,	8 24	..	9 24	..	1024	..	1124	..	1224	..	1 24	..	2 24	..	3 24
Mortimer	,,	8 30	..	9 30	..	1030	..	1130	..	1230	..	1 30	..	2 30	..	3 30
Reading West	,,	8 40	..	9 40	..	1040	..							2 40	..	3 40
Reading General	arr	8 43	..	9 43	..	1043	..	1141	..	1245	..	1 41	..	2 43	..	3 43

Up — Sundays—continued

		pm K		pm K		pm T		pm K		pm		pm R		pm R		pm		pm		pm R		pm K
32 Bournemouth West	.. dep	2 15	..	3 15	..	4P 5	..			5 15	..	6 35	..	7 0	..					
32 ,, Central	,,	2 27	..	3 35	..	4P14	..			5 25	..	6 45	..	7 10	..	8 15	..	8 58	
32 Southampton Central	,,	3 25	..	4 25	..	5 25	..	6 25	..	6 40	..	7 23	..	8 7	..	9 15	..	1030	
32 ,, Terminus	,,																		
32,54 Portsmouth & Southsea	,,	2 53	..	3 53	..	4 53	..	5 53	..			6 53	..	7 53	..	8 53	..	9 53	
35 Salisbury	,,	2 23	..					5 39	..			7 15	..			8 32			
Basingstoke	dep	4 17	..	5 17	..	6 17	..	7 19	..	7 45	..	8 21	..	9 18	..	9 40	..	1017	..	1122
Bramley	,,	4 26	..	5 24	..	6 24	..	7 26	..	7 52	..	8 28	..	9 25	..	9 47	..	1024	..	1129
Mortimer	,,	4 32	..	5 30	..	6 30	..	7 32	..	7 58	..	8 34	..	9 31	..	9 53	..	1030		
Reading West	,,	4 44	..	5 40	..	6 40	..	7 44	..	8 8	..	8 44	..	9 41	..	10 3	..			
Reading General	arr	4 47	..	5 43	..	6 43	..	7 47	..	8 11	..	8 47	..	9 44	..	10 6	..	1041	..	1145

K Through Train between Reading General and Southampton Central
N Through Train Reading General to Portsmouth Harbour, arr 10 39 am
P Passengers may dep Bournemouth West 4 30 pm, Bournemouth Cen. 4 40 pm, by Pullman Car Train (Supplementary fee payable) and change at Southampton Central

R Through Train between Reading General and Portsmouth & Southsea
T Through Train Fawley (dep 4 43 pm) (Tables 32 and 52) to Reading General
V Through Train Fawley (dep 7 44 am) (Tables 32 and 52) to Reading General
X Through Train Reading General to Eastleigh (arr 10 56 pm) (Table 32)

Z Through Train Reading General to Eastleigh (arr 11 49 pm) (Table 32)

d am. Monday mornings
e Via Eastleigh

Sunday service June-September 1962

65.   No. 6841 *Marlas Grange* approaches Bramley on 27th August 1955 with the 9.20am Birkenhead to Bournemouth train. An intermediate signal box (Stratfield Saye) between here and Mortimer was in use between 1917 and 1924, and another was provided between 1940 and 1950. They were built to help improve the flow of wartime military traffic. (S.C.Nash)

66.   Approaching Bramley on 18th May 1963 is ex-LNER no. 4472 *Flying Scotsman* with the Gainsborough Model Railway Society's special train from Lincoln to Southampton. A tour of the Isle of Wight was the objective. (S.C.Nash)

BRAMLEY

67. The station did not open until 1st May 1895 but it is clear that bridge rails and tie bars were still in use after that date. A single siding was provided here prior to the provision of passenger facilities. The number of residents increased slowly from about 500 in 1921 to 900 in 1931 and 1500 in 1951. (Lens of Sutton)

Bramley	1903	1913	1923	1933
Passenger tickets issued	16571	16956	26923	23203
Season tickets issued	-	-	196	122
Parcels forwarded	5488	13591	21390	5215
General goods forwarded (tons)	1351	2312	20648	4867
Coal and coke received	3278	2880	6640	5397
Other minerals received	833	574	3379	2842
General goods received	1431	2129	14091	3484
Trucks of livestock handled	24	90	59	16

68. This northward view shows that the bridge rails were drilled at intervals and secured direct to the timbers. At this early date, the crossing gates carried no warning "targets". "Bramley for Silchester" appeared in timetables for many years to avoid confusion with "Bramley & Wonersh" featured in our *Branch Lines to Horsham*. (Lens of Sutton)

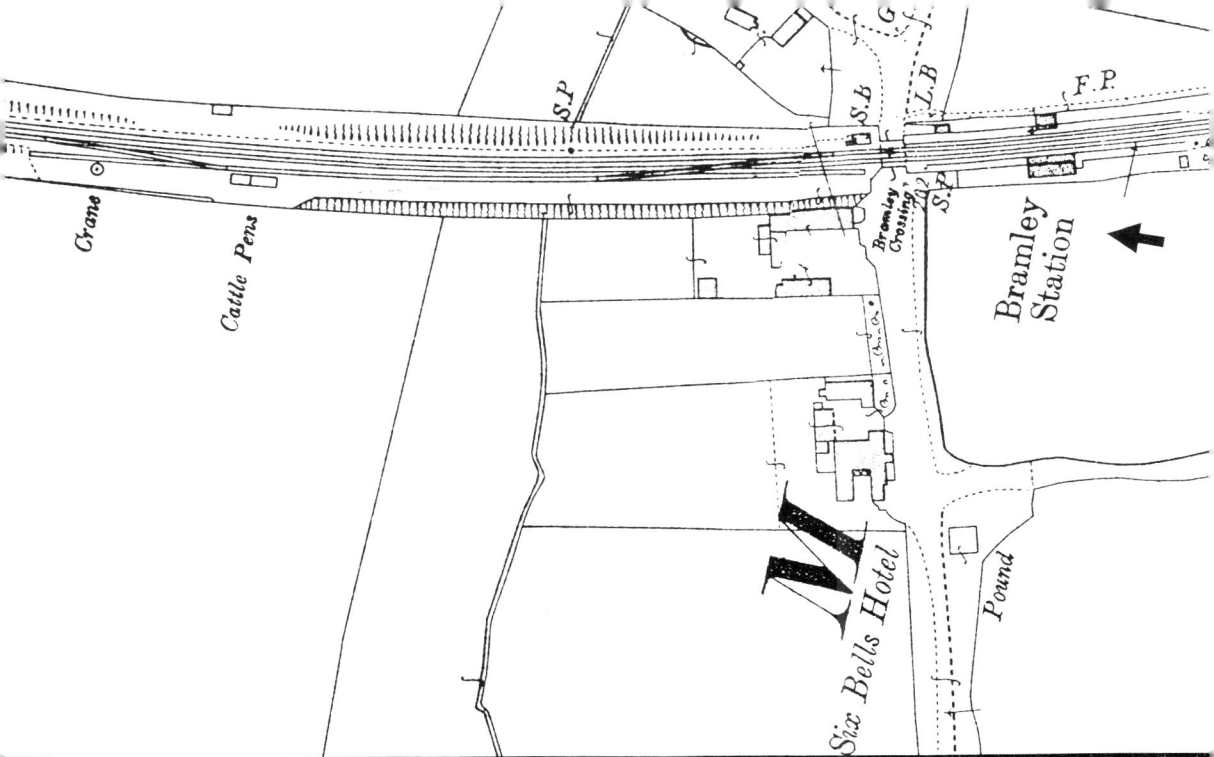

The 1911 map indicates the position of the
crane and cattle pens.

69.   Passing the goods yard on 27th August
1955 is the 10.15am Bradford to Poole, headed
by "King Arthur" class no. 30741 *Joyous Gard*.

This Saturdays-only train arrived at
Basingstoke at 4.17pm but did not stop at
either Reading station. (S.C.Nash)

70. The 1.3pm Reading to Basingstoke accelerates away from the station on the same day and passes the Army depot sidings. The locomotive, "King Arthur" class no. 30751 *Etarre* carries the normal diameter chimney unlike the one in the previous view. The sidings on the left had two connections to the munition works and were taken out of use in 1959. (S.C.Nash)

72. A rectangular yellow panel was a further step towards improving the sighting of the green DEMUs from the track. This April 1966 southward view of no. 1108 includes the signal for access to the Army sidings. (C.L.Caddy)

71. A 1966 photograph shows that the signal box had been relocated. This took place in 1917. Colour light signalling was commissioned from here northwards on 28th June 1964. A dramatic near collision had been staged close to the box in 1935 during the making of the film "The Last Journey". Twickenham Film Studios hired this part of the route from 9.30am to 8pm on two Sundays. (C.L.Caddy)

GREAT WESTERN RAILWAY

Nº 288

(ONE MONTH)
Rate £1 3 9

FROM

TO

BETWEEN

MORTIMER
AND
BASINGSTOKE

THIS TICKET IS TO BE GIVEN UP ON EXPIRY

73. The signal box was in use until 25th October 1977 and is seen shortly before closure. On that day automatic half barriers were brought into use to replace the level crossing gates. Colour light signals southwards were introduced on 20th November 1966. (J.Scrace)

74. Passing through the up platform on 6th July 1992 is no. 60033 with tankers of liquified petroleum gas from the Wytch Farm oilfield at Furzebrook (near Swanage) to Hallen Marsh (near Avonmouth) for export to Spain. Note that the station was still staffed. (P.G.Barnes)

75. Unofficially named *Lion*, no. 205032 runs past the site of the goods yard on 10th February 1993. Public freight facilities had been withdrawn on 7th January 1963 and the track was lifted in the following April. (M.J.Stretton)

Warning

Tickets
Waiting room
Ladies
Gentlemen

BRAMLEY M.O.D.

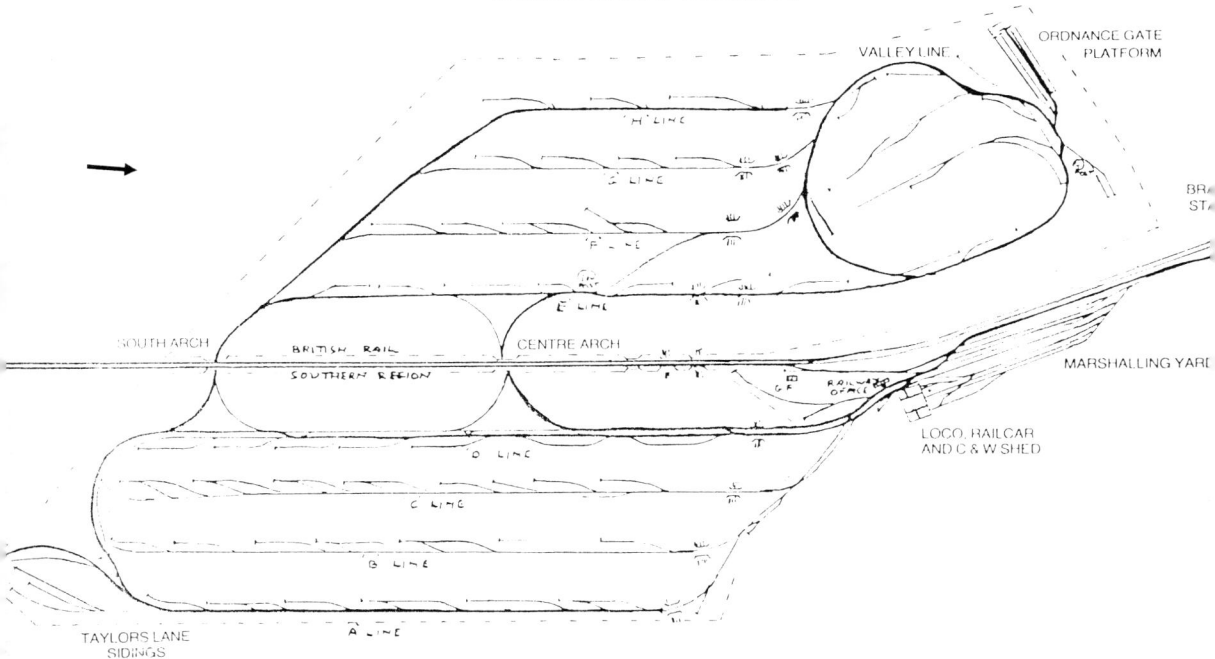

A munitions works and ordnance store was established south of Bramley station during World War I and by 1917 there were three sidings parallel to the up line and nine adjacent to the down. All were connected at both ends to the main lines and three lines (two on the up side and one on the down) passed through gates to the depot. The main line connections on the up side were lost in 1959 and that from the down line near Bramley station was removed in 1971.

The original six small second-hand steam locomotives were replaced in 1918-19 by new 0-6-0STs named Bramley nos. 1-7. In 1922-25, a number of these steam engines were displaced by four battery operated electric locomotives but steam power was increased by two more six-coupled tank engines in 1929. During the last war, with increasing activity at the depot, shunting locomotive reinforcements came from the GWR by the loan of several tank engines usually fitted with distinctive balloon spark arresters. Regulars were nos. 1912/25/69, others in the 5700 and 7700 series from Reading shed, some of the 1361 class and the ex-Barry Railway 0-6-0T no.

783. This was the situation until 1943, when the well known WD Austerity 0-6-0STs came to the Depot. By 1960, diesel mechanical locomotives had displaced the last of the steamers and the final allocation was three Rustons, nos. 421/2/35. The former steam locomotive shed was replaced by a diesel depot and workshops about 1960. The railway office and control room was adjacent to them.

In 1922 a set of eleven former North London Railway four-wheeled carriages were transferred from Longmoor. They were used for carrying employees on the internal services and for the morning and evening trains between Bramley station and the Depot main gate. The service was discontinued in about 1940 but was restarted in the 1950s using three ex-Piccadilly line tube coaches, WD 3022/3/4, which were equally suitable for negotiating sharp curves. At the end of the regular passenger service in about 1970, a Wickham railcar was the usual conveyance for the few personnel using the train from Reading. The diagram was issued to passengers on the "Bramley Bunker" on 1st March 1987, the bold line showing the route traversed.

76. Class 3H DEMU no. 1124 departs for Basingstoke on 9th August 1970 on the occasion of the RCTS visit to Bramley Military Railway. A Ruston Hornsby locomotive is coupled to ex-London Underground stock. The next six pictures were taken on the same day. (T.Wright)

77. The same train, complete with barrier wagons for coupling adaptation and a brake van, proceeds south past the locomotive depot. (T.Wright)

78.   This adapted Drewry railcar provided rapid response to a fire anywhere on the extensive site. Note the flashing lights and the traditional bell on the roof. This and no. 9112 had been converted at the depot's workshop. (T.Wright)

80.   Ammunition boxes form the background to this portrait of an antique 8-ton wagon adapted for water cartage. (T.Wright)

79.   Outside the running shed is Army 0-4-0 diesel no. 224 and 0-6-0 diesel hydraulic no. 223. As with most things military, cleanliness was paramount. (T.Wright)

81.   This 20-ton workshop van has a continental style and was probably reparation stock. The axleboxes are foreign. The vehicle was moved to the Army depot at Bicester in 1973, presumably devoid of the chimney which was out of gauge. (T.Wright)

The ticket for the tour carried an incorrect date as it had to be postponed 24 hours owing to engineering work on the main line.

82.   This was listed as being a "Side lift fork truck transporter" and having previously carried the numbers 958 and WGF040092. It is recorded as measuring 22ft. long and having been built at Ashford, although the appearance is of a shorter length. The buffers are of the distinctive continental self-contained pattern and with the assymetrical wheelbase give the impression that it might have been a rebuild of a foreign wagon. (T.Wright)

83.   This and the next three photographs were taken on one of the other rare occasions that the public was admitted to the site. This was on closure day, 1st March 1987, when two DEMUs toured much of the system. As there was no signalling, drivers simply had to keep a safe distance. The leading unit (205033) slipped to a standstill negotiating South Arch and had to back up for a second attempt. (R.E.Ruffell)

84. The second run was successful - the unit is seen after arrival at Ordnance Gate platform. This was probably the first and last time that BR passenger trains ran to this location. (R.E.Ruffell)

85. The problem of lack of platforms elsewhere was solved by means of steps. The low floor of the ex-Underground stock was a great advantage on this railway. This is one of Taylors Lane sidings. (M.P.Turvey)

86. Both DEMUs wait at Taylors Lane sidings while Ruston 0-6-0 Army no. 422 runs round the curve towards South Arch with a TV crew who recorded the event. The two units had run coupled from Basingstoke, departures being at 09.40, 12.40 and 15.40. (M.P.Turvey)

87. At its optimum there were 33 track miles and over 200 points. This is the desolate scene at the diesel depot ten years later. In 1993 there was an unsuccessful attempt to establish a transport museum here, although the connection to BR was still functional and many sidings were still in place, as was this substantial shed. (J.H.Bird)

SOUTH OF BRAMLEY

88.   The 11.16 Bournemouth to Newcastle is approaching Bramley on 27th August 1955 behind "King Arthur" class no. 30737 *King Uther*, which worked the train to Oxford. Bramley South box was behind the camera. It controlled access to the up sidings until their closure in 1959 and had been designated a ground frame since about 1924. (S.C.Nash)

89.   Seen on the same day, a Saturday, is ex-GWR 4300 class no. 7300 with the 1.30pm Portsmouth Harbour to Birmingham, not stopping at Reading. All available coaches were pressed into service for summer holiday traffic. (S.C.Nash)

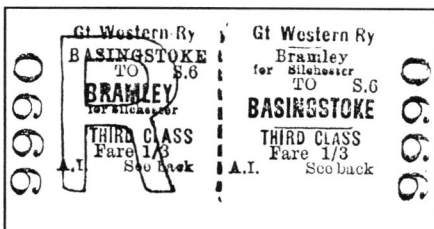

90.   With steam to spare and a malfunctioning injector, no. 30770 *Sir Prianius* accelerates away from Bramley on the same Saturday with the 1.48pm from Reading General. It was scheduled to stop for two minutes at Bramley and arrive at Portsmouth & Southsea at 4.7pm. (S.C.Nash)

91. No. 33104 with a 4TC set passes through the linear forest that embraces so many miles of railway in this age of lineside neglect. It is working the 16.00 Reading to Portsmouth Harbour on 24th May 1981 and will complete its journey at 17.48, 31 minutes quicker than in 1955 for a slightly longer journey to the Harbour terminus. (J.S.Petley)

October 1911

READING and BASINGSTOKE. Great Western.

Miles from Reading	Down.	Week Days.											Sundays.		
	Paddington Station.	mrn	mrn	mrn	aft	aft	aft	aft	aft	aft	aft		mrn	mrn	aft
2	London .... dep	7 30	9 0	10 50	12 40	1 45	3 18	4 50	5 47	7 30	9 15			9 20	4 55
2	Windsor and Eton ...	7 28	8 25	10 20	1 8	1 50	3 28	4 55	5 6	6 27	8 37			9 15	5 30
13	Oxford	8 0	9 5	10 41	9 1	1 50	4 52	4 8	4 25	4 47	5 6	9 24		7 25	4 47
	Reading .... dep	A 8 9	9 55	11 5	1 47	2 40	4 3	5 55	5 6	4 6	8 24	10 5		8 50	10 48 6 22
	Reading (West)	8 51	10 0	....	2 45	4 25	4 28	5 24	6 50	8 50				8 55	10 51 6 25
7	Mortimer	9 4	10 13	12 10	2 3	3 0	K	4 35	5 37	5 8	45	9 28		9 5	11 6 6 37
10	Bramley, for Silchester [159, 167]	9 11	10 20	12 17	2 10	3 7	...	4 55	5	4 47	10 8	50	H	9 12	11 14 6 48
15	Basingstoke 130. 136. arr	9 21	10 30	12 27	2 20	3 17	3 52	5 N 55	5 57	2 0	9 10	43		9 22	11 24 6 59

A Through Trains from Reading to Portsmouth, see pages 136 to 138. B Through Trains from Windsor and Eton to Basingstoke, see pages 5 and 7. F By Slip carriage. H Stops to set down from Reading and beyond on informing the Guard at Reading. K Stops to set down from Oxford and beyond on informing the Guard at Oxford. N Motor Car, one class only.

Map labels: Chineham Kiln Cottage · W · M.P · Kiln · Roman Pottery found · Gaston's Wood · S.P · 43 · 13·992 Sand Pit · GREAT · Daneshill Brick & Tile Works · Chy · Kiln · Kiln

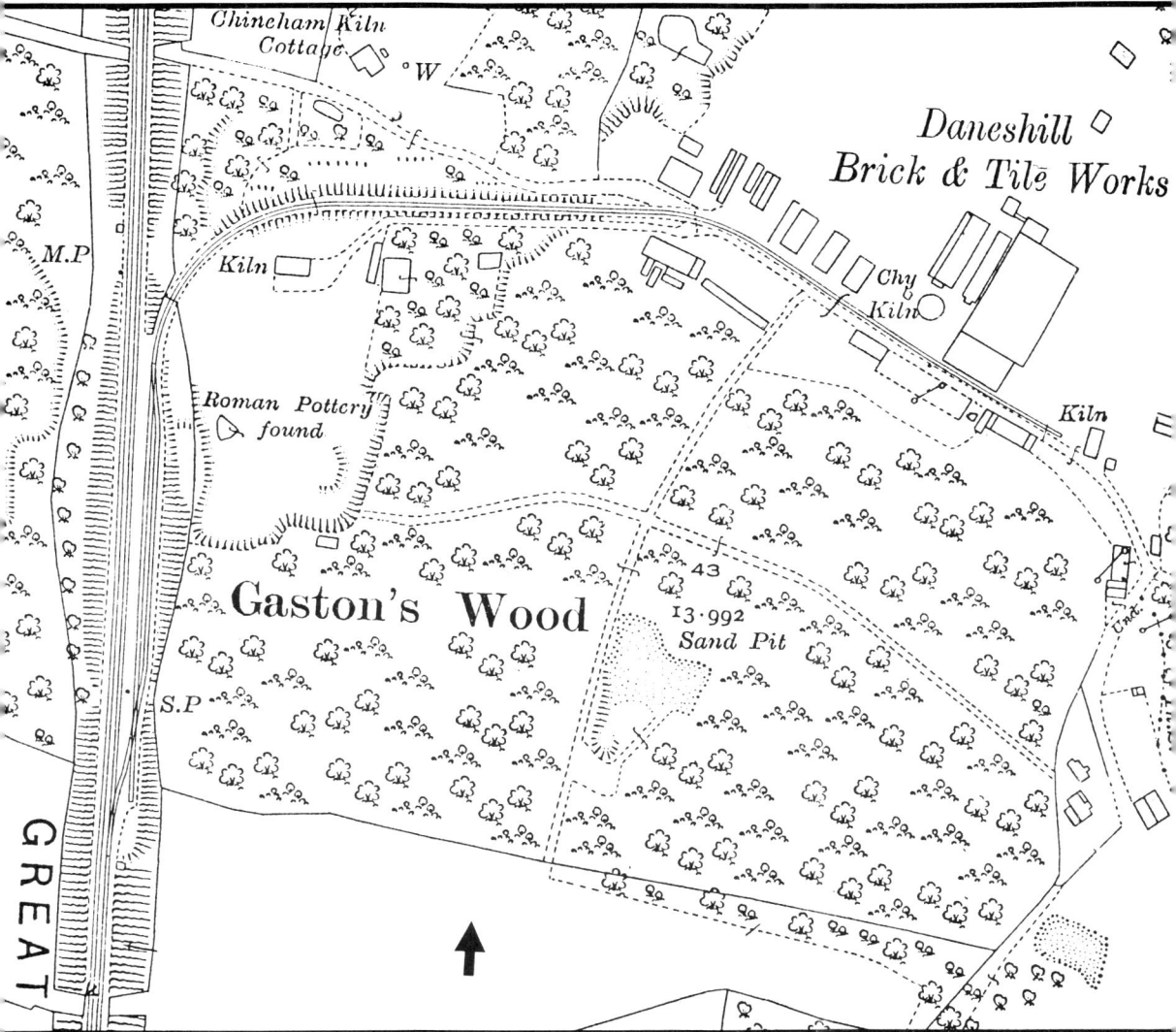

Slightly over a mile north of Basingstoke was the siding for Daneshill Brick & Tile Works. Just beyond the end of the loop is the gate to the private siding which was in use from 4th November 1908 to 31st December 1942. This map was surveyed in 1932.

BASINGSTOKE and READING. Great Western. (railway timetable)

92. Pannier tanks had few regular workings on the route but a 5700 class did sometimes work the 5.5pm from Reading. Here is no. 3740 of that class approaching Basingstoke on 24th June 1955. Three were shedded at Basingstoke in 1947. (R.C.Riley)

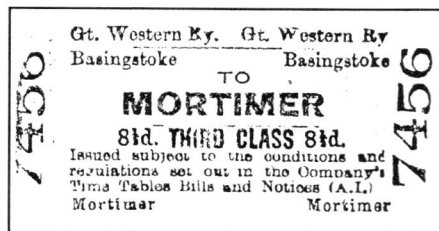

93. Class 5 no. 73037 leaves Basingstoke with a relief train from the South Coast on 14th August 1965, passing other holidaymakers destined for the seaside. The end of steam was nigh. The 1 in 255 gradient up to the station justified the catch points. (G.D.King)

94. The three-platform GWR terminus was adjacent to the LSWR station (left) but was separated from it by railings. It appears that the platform from which this photograph was taken had been widened since the broad gauge tracks had been lifted. The same roof design was employed at Westbury in 1848. (L.Waters coll.)

95. By 1920, these GWR platforms had been numbered 5, 6 and 7. In the distance is a wheeled drawbridge over the track at platform 6. This line gave a connection to the LSWR goods yard for freight transfer without using their main lines. Until 1856 a transfer shed was in use. (Lens of Sutton)

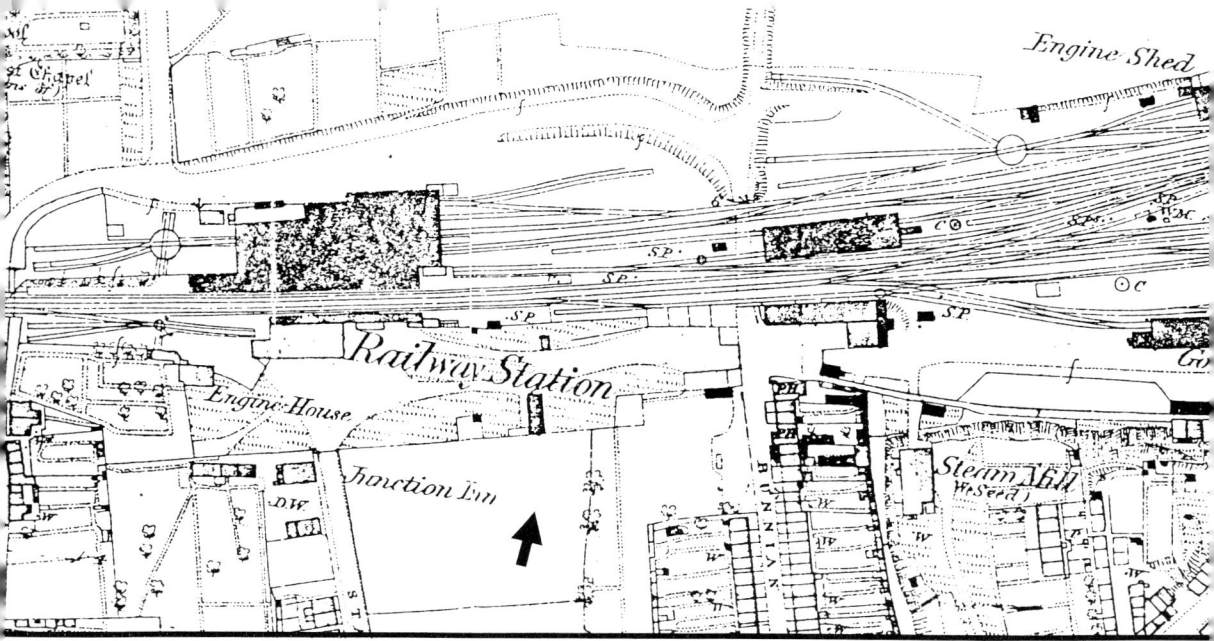

The goods transfer shed is in the centre of this 1872 map although it was not used for that purpose by that date.

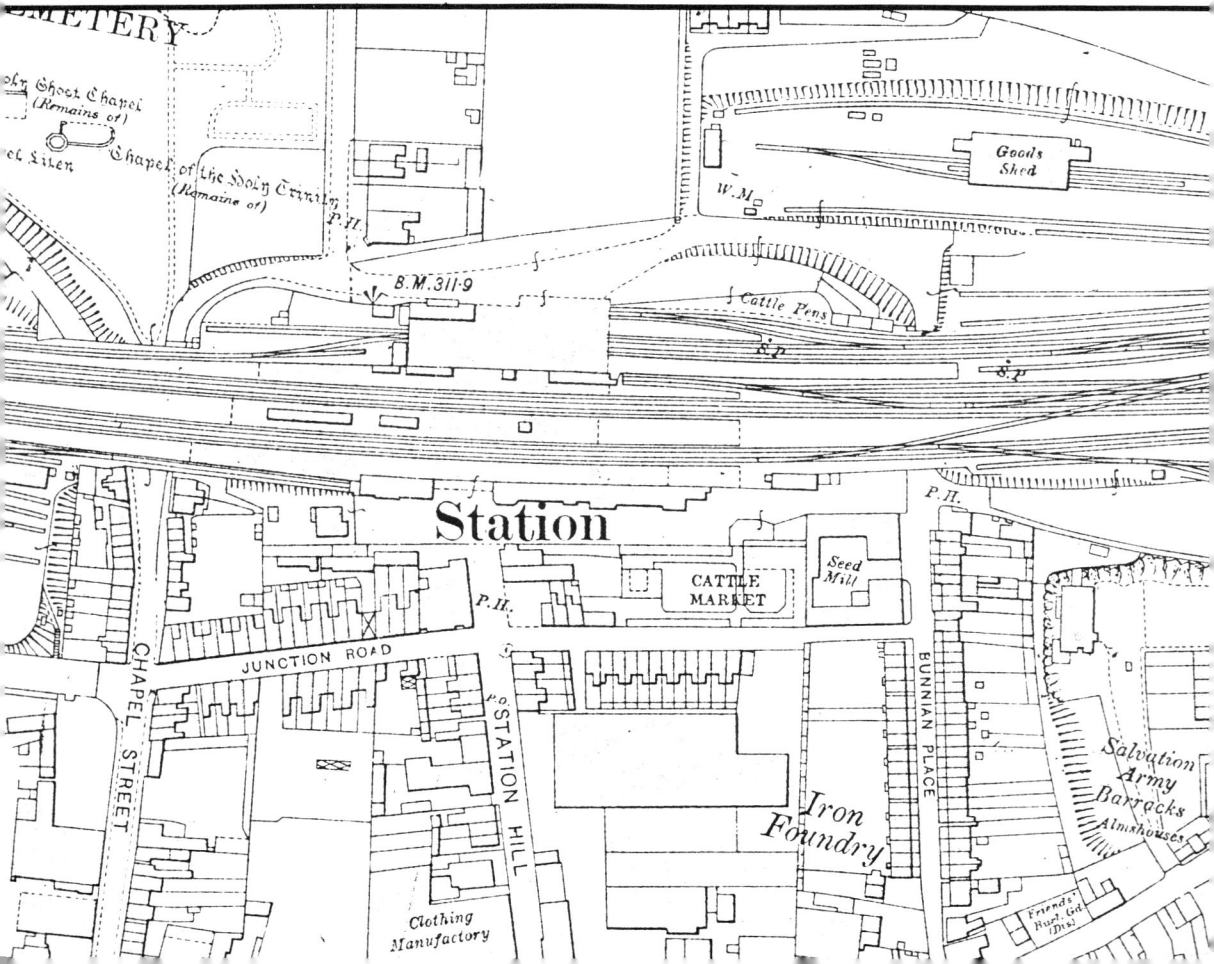

96. The GWR engine shed is marked on the map. It was in use until 26th November 1950 but the turntable had been removed in 1913. The south wall was of timber construction but brickwork was used at the north. (British Rail)

```
 2nd · SINGLE              SINGLE · 2nd
          Basingstoke to
 Basingstoke                    Basingstoke
 Ealing Broadway                Ealing Broadway
        EALING BROADWAY
             via Reading
 (S)          12/6  Fare  12/6        (S)
 For conditions see over  For conditions see over
```

The 1910 edition has the double track GWR route from Reading top right, with the LSWR's carriage sidings and Waterloo lines below.

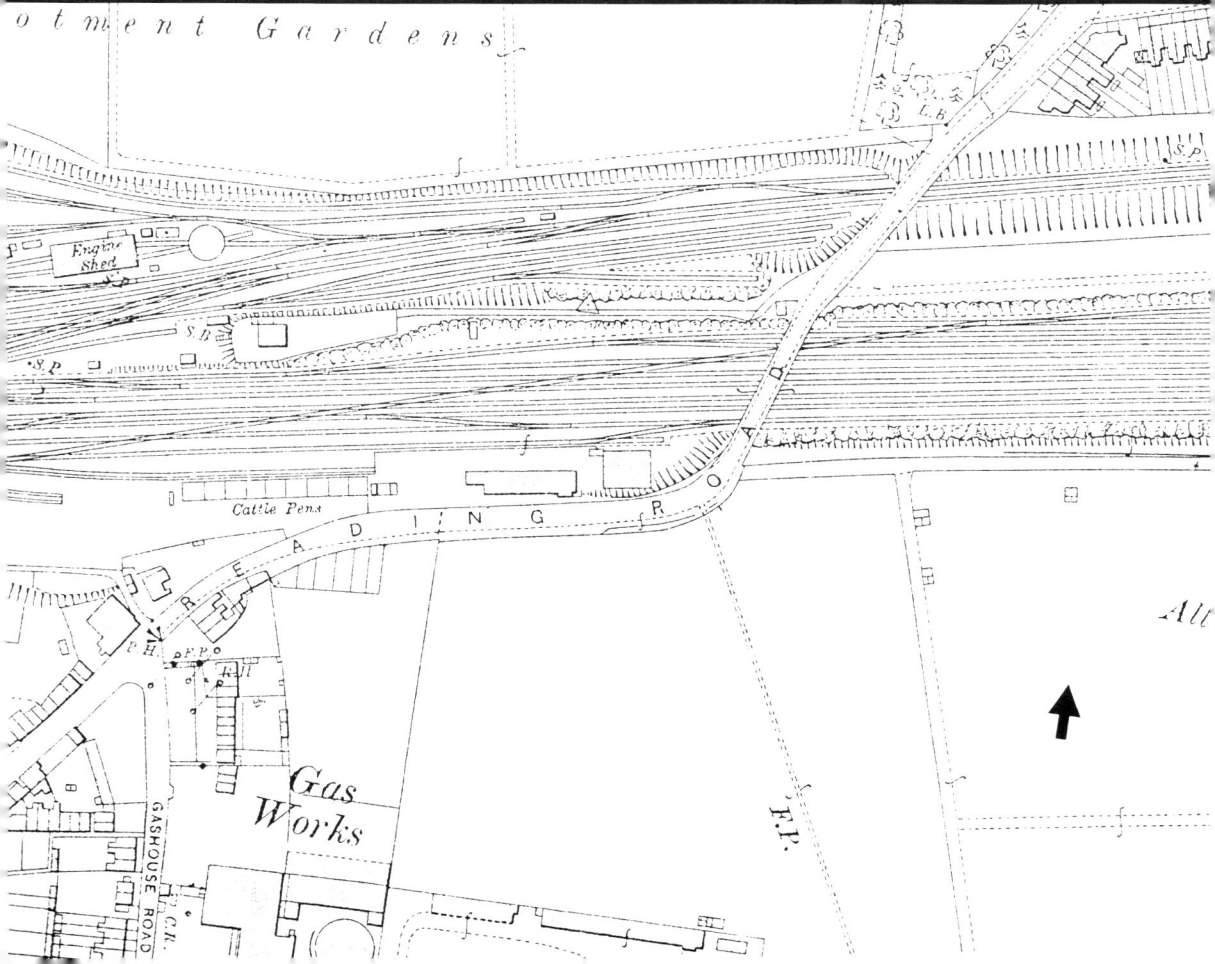

97.   Class 3521 no. 3556 approaches the terminus, the connections to the LSWR being on the right. Note the once popular clerestory coaches on the left of this view which is entirely GWR property. The locomotive was built in 1888 as a broad gauge convertible 0-4-2ST, became an 0-4-4ST in 1891, standard gauge in 1892 and a 4-4-0 in 1910. It was allocated to Reading in about 1919 and was scrapped in 1927. (Lens of Sutton)

SOUTHERN & GT. WESTERN RAILWAYS
BASINGSTOKE STATION

BOOKING OFFICE
SOUTHERN & G.W. RAILWAYS

98.   This photograph probably dates from 1940 as the platform lights have been removed due to the blackout restrictions but before station signs were removed as an enemy invasion precaution. The SR signals were pneumatically operated. (Lens of Sutton)

Gt. Western Ry.   Gt. Western Ry.
MORTIMER   MORTIMER
TO
PADDINGTON
7/2 FIRST CLASS 7/2
Issued subject to the conditions & regulations set out in the Company's Time Tables Books and Bills.   (O. G.)
Paddington   Paddington

99.   The exterior is seen in the mid-1950s at a time when there were many 30-year old cars still in use, an example being on the left. The joint signs remained for a long while after nationalisation. This was the third LSWR station on the site and was completed in about 1903. (H.C.Casserley coll.)

100.   Here is a closer view of the departure board seen in the previous picture. These were known as *Bencro* indicators and were manufactured by Benn & Cronin. The times were shown on small stove enamelled metal plates. The fluted bonnet belongs to a Vauxhall. (Lens of Sutton)

GREAT WESTERN RAILWAY
DIRECT ROUTE TO

LIVERPOOL. MANCHESTER. CREWE & NORTH OF ENGLAND. CHESTER. HOLYHEAD.
DUBLIN & NORTH OF IRELAND. BIRMINGHAM. WOLVERHAMPTON.
SHREWSBURY & NORTH WALES. WORCESTER. HEREFORD. GLOUCESTER. &
SOUTH WALES. BATH. BRISTOL. LEAMINGTON. CHELTENHAM. WARWICK.
CARDIFF. FISHGUARD. ROSSLARE. CORK & SOUTH OF IRELAND.

WAY OUT ➤➤
& PLATFORMS 3. 2 & 1

101. This is the boundary wall between the two stations, recorded on 26th April 1953. The *DIRECT ROUTE* is something of an over-statement. The timber clad building is in the centre of picture 95 and was eventually used as a railway staff club. GWR staffing ceased on 1st January 1932. (D.Cullum)

102. No. 5966 *Asford Hall* is piloting no. 7900 *Saint Peters Hall* on 13th August 1960, the latter probably being in poor health. The train is bound for Portsmouth & Southsea and is crossing to the former LSWR main line. (T.Wright)

103.   The ex-GWR signal box was still in use when no. 30858 *Lord Duncan* passed by on 4th March 1961. The train left Bournemouth West at 11.16am, was due at York at 7.42pm and ran via Banbury General, Loughborough Central and Nottingham Victoria. (A.G.Thorpe)

104.   Class N15 no. 30768 approaches the junction with an inter-regional freight, the brake van being at the top of the incline. The photograph was taken on 4th March 1961. The sidings on the right were taken out of use on 8th August 1965. (A.G.Thorpe)

105. The bridge in the previous picture is also in the background of this one. A DEMU with a V warning pattern is working a Reading-Southampton service on 14th October 1962 while the signal is off for an up train for the Reading line. "A" Box is on the right. (A.E.Bennett)

106. The Railway Enthusiasts Club of Farnborough operated this railtour on 23rd March 1963 which was recorded at the remains of platform 6. The trip included the Bulford branch, the Didcot & Newbury line, Reading Central Goods and Ascot. (A.E.Bennett)

Gt. Western Ry.   Gt. Western Ry.
MORTIMER   MORTIMER
TO
READING
1/2 FIRST CLASS 1/2
Issued subject to the conditions & regu
lations set out in the Company's Time
Tables Books and Bills.   (O. G.)
Reading   Reading

107. After closure of the Western Region shed in 1950 their locomotives were serviced at the Southern Region shed (left). Unnamed "Hall" class no. 6923 (formerly *Croxteth Hall*) was photographed west of the station on 20th July 1963. (D.Tuck)

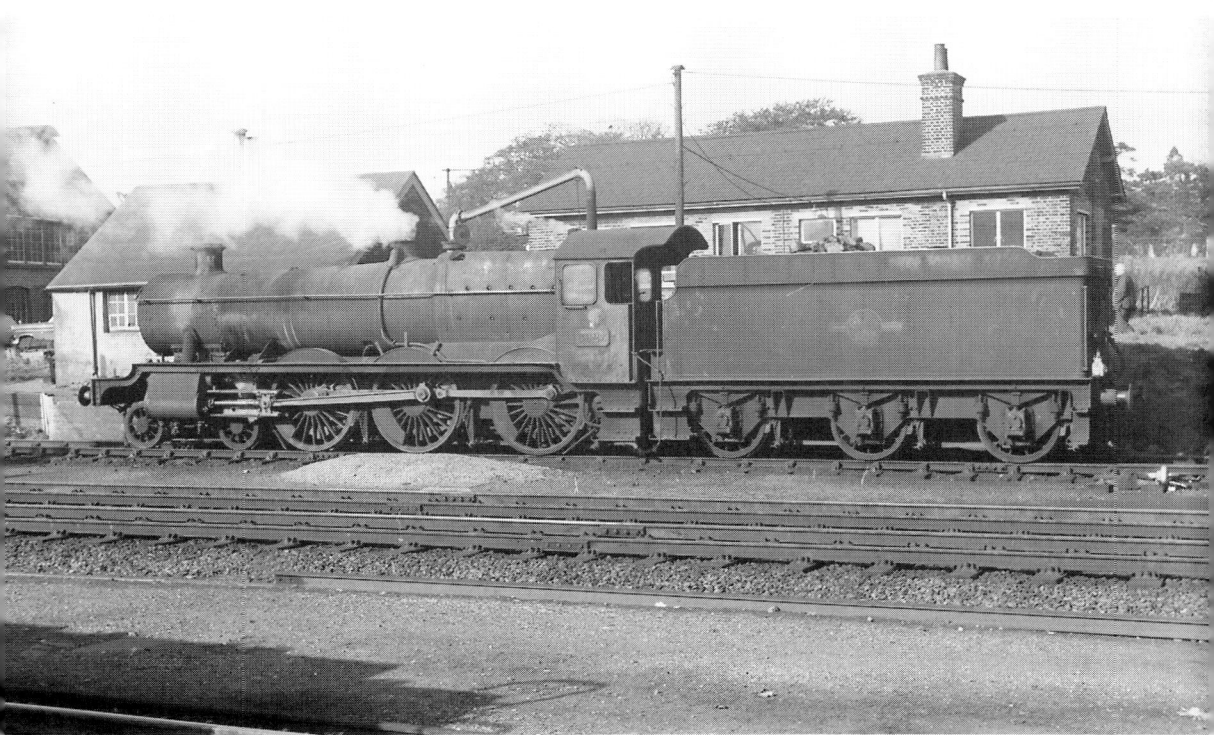

108. As picture 106 also shows, there were two through lines after the demolition of the overall roof, these converging into the one on which the locomotive is standing in the previous picture. Class U no. 31800 is working through platform 5 on 1st July 1963. (H.C.Casserley)

109. Stops were placed at the end of platform 5 on 26th March 1965, no. 6 road thereafter being used for freight. On the left is the building seen on the right of picture 95. (C.L.Caddy)

110. The three Basingstoke signal boxes were designated A, B and C on 27th May 1956 and were all closed on 20th November 1966, when the nearby panel box came into use. This is the former GWR box, photographed in 1965 and seen earlier in pictures 97 and 103. The brick base was still evident in 1994. (J.J.Smith)

111. On the right, "The Great Western" stands as a memorial to the golden age of steam and pride in an integrated system. A class 3H DEMU throbs in the one remaining bay platform before returning to Reading on 21st June 1980. (F.Hornby)

Gt. Western Ry.
PRIVILEGE
Mortimer to
BASINGSTOKE
THIRD CLASS
Fare 11d Z
CL SEE BACK
715

Gt. Western Ry.
PRIVILEGE
BASINGSTOKE to
MORTIMER
THIRD CLASS
Fare 11d Z
CL SEE BACK
715

2nd - SINGLE   SINGLE - 2nd
(5500A)   (5500A)
Mortimer to
Mortimer   Mortimer
Basingstoke   Basingstoke
BASINGSTOKE
(S)   18p Fare 18p   (S)
For conditions see ove For conditions see over
0328   0328

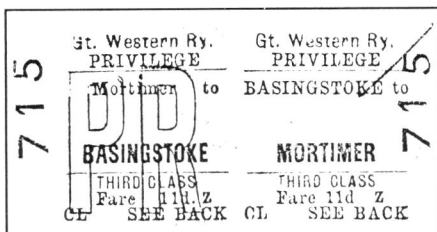

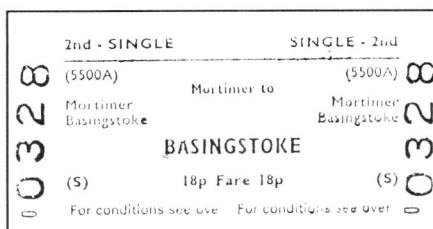

112. Part of the boundary railings remained on 22nd August 1981 as no. 47228 waits to run on to the Reading line with a Poole to Manchester Piccadilly train. Early BR Mk.I coaches are in evidence, their life by then limited. (T.Heavyside)

113. Inter-regional freight has also made up a large part of the traffic on the route. No. 33119 is about to turn onto the Reading line with assorted wagons on 8th March 1982. Freight working with a class 33/1 was fairly unusual. (J.S.Petley)

114. Inter-regional passenger trains have traversed the route every two hours during weekdays for many years. No. 47350 accelerates the 09.03 Poole to Liverpool train on 7th September 1985. Class 47/3s lack electric train heating equipment but could be used on summer services. (J.S.Petley)

115. The combined trains seen in pictures 83 to 86 wait to depart from platform 5 at 12.40 on 1st March 1987. The event proved so popular that there were many standing passengers. The 1966 Basingstoke panel box is in the background, in the V of the junction. (M.P.Turvey)

116.   On 2nd March 1987, Army diesels nos. 435, 421 and 422, together with two former BR(S) brake vans, left Bramley at 09.20. They are shown passing through Basingstoke en route to the Army depot at Ludgershall. (R.E.Ruffell)

117.   Much of the export trade from the Midlands and North of England is shipped from Southampton, the containers traversing the route at regular intervals, day and night. No. 47290 was photographed from platform 4 on 25th September 1991. (J.Scrace)

118. Owing to a shortage of locomotives on the Waterloo-Exeter route, a number of DEMU workings from Reading were extended to Salisbury in 1991-93 to provide a local service. No. 207013 was one of the 3D sets built for the Oxted area services and is seen coupled to two coaches of earlier livery, bound for Salisbury on 28th November 1992. (P.G.Barnes)

The development of the southern side of the station is illustrated in the companion albums *Basingstoke to Salisbury, Woking to Southampton* and *Branch Lines to Alton*, all by the same authors and publisher.

119. Turbo no. 165131 stands quietly at platform 5 on 3rd August 1993 while a stopping train from Waterloo terminates in platform 1. The station had been refurbished in a partnership scheme with a local firm, Provident Life. (V.Mitchell)

120. The outer ends of three sidings had been retained by the engineers, most of the remainder of the GWR site becoming a car park. No. 165009 works the 11.35 to Reading on 5th June 1993, helping to provide a useful half-hourly service between one of the principal towns of Hampshire and the county town of Berkshire. (C.Wilson)

MP Middleton Press

Easebourne Lane, Midhurst. West Sussex. GU29 9AZ   Tel: (0730) 813169 Fax: (0730) 812601
. . . . . Write or telephone for our latest list . . . . .

BRANCH LINES

Branch Line to Allhallows
Branch Lines to Alton
Branch Lines tround Ascot
Branch Lines to East Grinstead
Branch Lines tround Effingham Jn
Branch Lines to Exmouth
Branch Line to Fairford
Branch Lines around Gosport
Branch Line to Hawkhurst
Branch Line to Hayling
Branch Lines to Horsham
Branch Lines around Huntingdon
Branch Lines to Ilfracombe
Branch Lines to Longmoor
Branch Line to Lyme Regis
Branch Line to Lynton
Branch Lines around March
Branch Lines around Midhurst
Branch Line to Minehead
Branch Lines to Newport
Branch Lines around Portmadoc (1923-46)
Branch Lines to Seaton & Sidmouth
Branch Line to Selsey
Branch Lines around Sheerness
Branch Line to Shrewsbury
Branch Line to Southwold
Branch Line to Swanage
Branch Line to Tenterden
Branch Lines to Tunbridge Wells
Branch Lines tround Weymouth
Branch Lines around Wimborne

LONDON SUBURBAN RAILWAYS

Caterham and Tattenham Corner
Charing Cross to Dartford
Crystal Palace and Catford Loop
Holborn Viaduct to Lewisham
Kingston and Hounslow Loops
Lewisham to Dartford
London Bridge to Addiscombe
Mitcham Junction Lines
West Croydon to Epsom

STEAMING THROUGH

Steaming through East Hants
Steaming through the Isle of Wight
Steaming through Surrey
Steaming through West Hants
Steaming through West Sussex

SOUTH COAST RAILWAYS

Ashford to Dover
Bournemouth to Weymouth
Brighton to Eastbourne
Brighton to Worthing
Chichester to Portsmouth
Dover to Ramsgate
Eastbourne to Hastings
Hastings to Ashford
Southampton to Bournemouth

SOUTHERN MAIN LINES

Basingstoke to Salisbury
Bromley South to Rochester
Charing Cross to Orpington
Crawley to Littlehampton
East Croydon to Three Bridges
Epsom to Horsham
Exeter to Barnstaple
Faversham to Dover
Haywards Heath to Seaford
London Bridge to East Croydon
Orpington to Tonbridge
Salisbury to Yeovil
Sittingbourne to Ramsgate
Three Bridges to Brighton
Tonbridge to Hastings
Victoria to Bromley South
Victoria to East Croydon
Waterloo to Windsor
Waterloo to Woking
Woking to Southampton
Yeovil to Exeter

COUNTRY RAILWAY ROUTES

Andover to Southampton
Bath To Evercreech Junction
Bournemouth to Evercreech Jn
Burnham to Evercreech Junction
East Kent Light Railway
Fareham to Salisbury
Guildford to Redhill
Reading to Guildford
Redhill to Ashford
Strood to Paddock Wood
Woking to Alton
Yeovil to Dorchester

TRAMWAY CLASSICS

Brighton's Tramways
Camberwell & W. Norwood Tramways
Dover's Tramways
Greenwich & Dartford Tramways
Hastings Tramways
Thanet's Tramways

BUS BOOKS

Eastbourne Bus Story
Tillingbourne Bus Story

OTHER RAILWAY BOOKS

Garraway Father & Son
Industrial Railways of the South East
London Chatham & Dover Railway
South Eastern Railway
War on the Line
West Sussex Railways in the 1980s

MILITARY BOOKS

Battle Over Portsmouth
Battle Over Sussex 1940
Military Defence of West Sussex

WATERWAY ALBUMS

Hampshire Waterways
Kent and East Sussex Waterways
West Sussex Waterways

COUNTRY BOOKS

Betwixt Petersfield and Midhurst
Brickmaking in Sussex
East Grinstead Then and Now
Leigh Park
Walking Ashdown Forest